CHINA'S HARVEST FIELDS

CHINA'S HARVEST FIELDS

TABOR LAUGHLIN

RESOURCE *Publications* • Eugene, Oregon

CHINA'S HARVEST FIELDS

Copyright © 2020 Tabor Laughlin. All rights reserved. Except for brief quotations in critical publications or reviews, no part of this book may be reproduced in any manner without prior written permission from the publisher. Write: Permissions, Wipf and Stock Publishers, 199 W. 8th Ave., Suite 3, Eugene, OR 97401.

Resource Publications
An Imprint of Wipf and Stock Publishers
199 W. 8th Ave., Suite 3
Eugene, OR 97401

www.wipfandstock.com

PAPERBACK ISBN: 978-1-7252-6091-7
HARDCOVER ISBN: 978-1-7252-6089-4
EBOOK ISBN: 978-1-7252-6090-0

Manufactured in the U.S.A.   04/01/20

To all those Chinese and missionaries who have ministered in Mainland China over the centuries, sometimes within a context of great persecution and oppression from the Chinese government.

"The harvest is plentiful but the workers are few. Ask the Lord of the harvest, therefore, to send out workers into his harvest field."

(MATTHEW 9:37, 38)

Contents

Introduction ix
TABOR LAUGHLIN

PART I: IMPACTING URBAN AND INFLUENTIAL CHINESE

CHAPTER 1   3
Reaching Big Cities
BRENT FULTON

CHAPTER 2   18
Foreign Business Leaders Using Kingdom Values to Transform the Workplace
ELISABETH KIM

CHAPTER 3   25
Reaching Educated Chinese through Teaching English
TABOR LAUGHLIN

PART II: SOCIAL IMPACT ON CHINESE SOCIETY

CHAPTER 4   33
Bioethics, Abortion and Missions in China
JOHN ENSOR

CHAPTER 5   47
Social Service Ministry in China
SWELLS IN THE MIDDLE KINGDOM

CHAPTER 6   65
Reaching China through Caring for Marginalized People
J. HADDON BENNETT

PART III: IMPACTING CHINESE HOUSE CHURCHES

CHAPTER 7 — 81
Missionaries reaching Chinese theologically (especially through seminaries)
ALLEN YEH

CHAPTER 8 — 91
Missionaries' Role in Theological Education in China
URBAN FARMER

CHAPTER 9 — 101
Helping Chinese House Churches Towards Spiritual Growth and Discipleship
G. WRIGHT DOYLE

PART IV: OTHER KEY COMPONENTS IN CHINA'S HARVEST FIELDS

CHAPTER 10 — 121
A Humble and Sacrificial Mission
CHEN JING

CHAPTER 11 — 130
Missionaries Helping Local Churches Reach Unreached People Groups
BARNABAS ROLAND

CHAPTER 12 — 141
Reaching Northwest China
TABOR LAUGHLIN

Bibliography — 147

Introduction

TABOR LAUGHLIN

Many of us are familiar with the existence of many Christians and house churches in present day China. How did this happen? Giving a brief history, the gospel first arrived in China many centuries ago. The first known missionaries to China were the Nestorians in the 600s. They made it all the way to the modern-day city Xi'an in NW China, and made good relationships with the emperor of the Tang Dynasty. In the 1800s, China received missionaries from Western countries, most notable of who were Robert Morrison and Hudson Taylor. Morrison was the first modern missionary in China and helped translate the Bible into Chinese. And Taylor is well known for his founding of the China Inland Mission, which led to hundreds of missionaries moving to inland China. And up to the present day, missionaries and local Chinese have spread the gospel across China.

This book highlights the many facets of ministry needs that continue to be prevalent within China. The intent is that this book will help missionaries and Chinese house churches to be better equipped to meet the multidimensional ministry facets existing within present day China. Each chapter has two emphases. One emphasis in each chapter is to look at the different outreach needs existing within China. The second emphasis is to consider how the ministry need focused on in that chapter can be passed on to the Chinese churches, that Chinese believers may be spurred on to be more involved in reaching that outreach need. A large goal is that the Chinese church may be standing firm on their own and flourishing without outside help from missionaries.

How can the gospel become most permeated within the country of China? The answer to this question is not related to simply improving theological education in China, or seeing Chinese Christians in the workplace truly impacting their companies and communities. Though these are factors, the current ministry in China is multi-faceted. Similarly, the needs of the Chinese church in standing on their own apart from help from foreigners also has multiple dimensions. And this is a big part of what this book is about, to look at the numerous factors involved with reaching China, and the factors of a "strong" Chinese church body standing up for the years to come.

PRESENT SITUATION OF CHRISTIANITY IN CHINA

For those of us who have or who are or who will minister to people in China, it is important to have a good understanding of the present state of the Chinese church in Mainland China. For the last thirty or forty years, Christianity in China has exploded. At present, there are two kinds of churches. The most common type of church in China is the "house church." These do not necessarily meet in homes, but often in office buildings or large apartments. We can assume that all "house churches" are in a home, and consist of just a handful of people. This is usually not the case, particularly for house churches in cities. Some house churches in recent years may have over a thousand people attending on a Sunday morning. House churches are illegal. They do not have any official connection with the government.

The other kind of church in China is the government church, or "Three-Self church." The Three-Self church is officially registered with the Chinese Communist government. The Three-Self church is legal and meets in a church building that is visible to the public. There are many more Chinese Christians in house churches than there are in Three-Self churches. Some assume that Three-Self churches are more likely to be heretical since they are connected to the Communist Party, while house churches are vibrant and biblical. This is not always the case, as there are many heretical house churches and many biblically sound Three-Self churches that focus on evangelism.

Churches in rural areas are often charismatic. And there are some rural areas in China that have a very high percentage of Christians. Urban house churches that are led by poor and uneducated Christians from rural areas are often also charismatic. But, urban house churches led by well-educated pastors are less likely to be charismatic. These house churches would have a higher percentage of college-educated believers, while house churches in rural areas would have very few high school or college graduates.

As for the number of Christians in China, different people say different things. From my ten years of living in China, living in eastern China, central China, and western China, my estimate is not that the Chinese Christian population is as high as 100 million as some speculate. Rather, my estimate of genuine "born-again" believers in China would be closer to 50 million total Christians, which corresponds to Lian Xi's estimation in his 2009 book Redeemed by Fire. This estimate of Christians in China is what all the contributors in this book use.

PERSECUTION OF CHRISTIANS IN CHINA?

Another question related to Chinese Christianity and missionaries living in China is: How real is the oppression of Chinese Christians and missionaries by the Chinese Communist government? Christianity is not illegal, but all churches in China legally must register with the government. These registered churches are the Three-Self churches. All house churches in China—which are the bulk of Chinese Christians—are illegal. So Christianity in China is strongly controlled. Many of us are familiar with how heavily the Chinese Christians were persecuted during Chairman Mao's reign, and particularly during the Cultural Revolution from 1966–1976. Many Christians during this time were imprisoned, sent to labor camps, tortured, pressured to deny their faith, or killed by the Communist guards. Through the power of the Holy Spirit, the Chinese church was able to grow and spread amidst this intense persecution. This hidden spiritual fervor during the Cultural Revolution was partly what led to a huge spreading of Christianity in the decades following China's re-opening to the outside world in 1979 after Chairman Mao's death.

All of this being the case, what is the state of the persecution of Christians in the modern day? Are Christians in China still put in prison, sent to labor camps, or killed for their faith, as was the case during the Cultural Revolution? Christians worldwide are surprised to hear that in China most house church Christians—technically "illegal" Christians—live their lives with very little interference from the police or other Communist authorities. Chinese Christians go to house churches on Sunday mornings. They do this every week, week after week, year after year, with usually no Chinese police barging in to arrest people and burn down the church. Particularly with those from the majority people group (Han) in China, Han Christians in China worship and live out their Christian faith with few limitations. If a house church pastor belongs to a minority ethnic group (i.e. Uyghur in NW China), then the Chinese government will be more likely to arrest them and throw them into prison longer-term.

In the last few years, there have been policies from Chinese President Xi Jinping that seem to indicate more oppression of Chinese Christians. However, as is often the case with policies in China, just because the policy exists does not mean that the policy will be enforced all around China. In other words, though the policy exists, this does not mean that suddenly all house church Christians will be put into prison, or all house churches will be shut down, or that all missionaries in China will be kicked out. Actually, it is very rare for Chinese Christians to be put in prison, unless just for a day or two to warn local house church leaders every once in a while. Recently a Chinese pastor Wang Yi was sentenced to nine years in prison for his outspoken opposition to the oppression of house churches by the Chinese government. Wang Yi's arrest and long imprisonment is not a normal case for house church pastors in China, but rather an exception. Additionally, the past few years, there have been some Three-Self churches in eastern China that have had crosses destroyed on their church building by the local government. And beginning in 2018 there has been a wider persecution of Christians throughout China, but usually it just entails the government splitting up larger house churches into smaller groups.

For those of us who are or have been missionaries in China, sometimes we may feel like we are always being watched by the local Chinese police. In general, though, missionaries in China—like Chinese Christians in China—live their lives with very little interference from the government. It is easier for missionaries to blend in living in a larger city, as there are many other foreigners in larger cities. Living in a smaller city makes it nearly impossible to blend in or fly under the radar with the local authorities. Nonetheless, oftentimes the ministry needs for missionaries can be greater in smaller cities where other missionaries are less likely to go. Because China is a "closed" country and it is illegal to be a missionary and impossible to have a "missionary" visa, missionaries in China must have some other form of visa, like a work or student visa.

During my ten years in China, we have never regularly attended a local Chinese house church. Though some missionaries in China attend Chinese house churches, we have not found this to be a good idea. It is entirely too dangerous usually for the Chinese Christians themselves for foreigners to attend, and also dangerous for us as foreigners. It has been more prudent for us to go to foreigner churches, which are either very small and in one of our apartments, or may be a larger international church gathering in a specifically rented out facility. Also, we have found that weekly going to a church in our first language, English, is spiritually much more encouraging and beneficial than trying to regularly attend church in only our second language, Chinese, and not regularly having a church group in English. Though some missionaries in China are involved in planting local Chinese house churches, we have found for us cooperating in other ways with the already existing local house churches is better than us trying to plant new Chinese house churches, as most areas all around China have several Chinese house churches relatively nearby.

THIS BOOK

A question that Christians globally ask is about the church in China, and the thousands of missionaries and house churches there. The book aims to look at the current ways that missionaries and local Chinese believers can minister in China, while also highlighting ways for the Chinese church to be stronger and able to sustain and flourish long-term apart from help from missionaries. Now many outreach needs continue to exist within China, which are highlighted in each chapter of this book.

I have not seen another book about China that covers so many topics as are in this book. And the topics are relevant and practical to the ministry efforts in China. This book includes multiple authors contributing to the book, all bringing their own expertise. Some of these authors are professors at large seminaries in the U.S. Some are missionaries or professionals in China, serving in various ways. Some are leaders of mission organizations in China. So there are different perspectives going into this book to give the reader a holistic view of the mission efforts in China.

As for the layout of this book, the first section of the book focuses on reaching wealthy Chinese in cities and the more prominent people within the Chinese society. The second section is intended to give a picture of ways that missionaries and Chinese Christians can meet social needs within the Chinese community. The third part of the book pertains to how missionaries and Chinese can help in seeing healthy and flourishing house churches and local Chinese seminaries. And the last part of the book explains how those ministering within China can reach other key outreach components within China: western China, unreached people groups, and mobilizing Chinese missionaries to reach the nations.

The topics in this book are not just abstract and theoretical topics to discuss, but are intended to have a tangible and practical impact on mission efforts in China. The book aims to go beyond the surface level understanding of ministry in China, and to dig much deeper into particulars of outreach needs in China. This book should be of benefit for missionaries and house churches within China, as the book displays the diversity of ministry needs in China. An additional hope in this book is that Christians worldwide who are interested in the Chinese church and missionaries in China may gain a more accurate perspective of what is actually happening with ministry within China.

PART I

Impacting Urban and
Influential Chinese

Chapter 1

Reaching Big Cities

BRENT FULTON

The return of foreign Christian workers to China in the 1980s and 90s coincided with the most massive peacetime human migration in the history of the world, as China transformed from a rural, agrarian society to a nation having more than half of its population in the cities. While not all foreign Christians served in urban areas, a majority did, and their presence proved instrumental in the development of the church, which, like the population at large, was also experiencing a major transformation.

From a largely marginalized peasant movement, the church today has emerged as a significant and increasingly influential group within China's rapidly changing urban society.

No longer merely in "survival mode," China's Christians have gone beyond meeting immediate needs for Bibles and training to address longer term questions of church life and organization. A pietistic, other-worldly orientation is giving way to greater social engagement. New forms of witness and outreach that were unthinkable at the end of the last century have been made possible as Christians claimed new territory in the marketplace, on campuses, and in cyberspace. Younger leaders—many of them first-generation believers who have studied or worked abroad—are breaking new ground theologically as they wrestle with the church's identity in a complex environment that blends free market capitalism with authoritarian rule.

Central to the remarkable growth of the urban church has been the role of foreign Christians, many whose presence predates the massive urban migration and who have played a vital role in evangelization, facilitation, and resourcing the church. Now as the urban church comes into its own, and as China becomes less hospitable to outside actors, the role of the foreigner is changing, necessitating a fresh intentionality in "passing the baton" to local Christian leaders who are taking the church forward in new directions.

BUILDING AND CONNECTING IN CHINA'S CITIES

China's urbanization made possible sustained double-digit economic growth into the first decade of this century. By 2010 China's middle class accounted for 12 percent of the total population. It is expected to double from 2011–21.[1] On the other end of the economic spectrum, China has lifted an estimated 300 million out of poverty, many of them migrants who have flocked to the cities in search of a better life.[2]

Sociologist Mary Ma describes the wave of migration that ensued as China embraced its reform and opening policy beginning in the 1980s:

"As a result of gradual deregulation, the number of rural workers migrating from their villages tripled from 20 million to 60 million within less than a decade until the early 1990s. In the following decade, China's landscape witnessed the biggest peacetime wave of internal migration the world has ever seen. By 2007, half of the Chinese population became city-dwellers, compared to just 20 percent in 1985."[3]

This migration has proceeded along a burgeoning network of roads and railways that have drawn China's cities closer together, enabling the acceleration of commerce to fuel China's rapid economic rise. Myriad new airports have sprung up since the 1980s, linking cities and providing gateways for those coming to China for work, study, tourism, or to reconnect with family members from who they had been separated for a generation or more.

On university campuses across China, West and East have come together in the classroom through the presence of foreign English teachers—a large proportion of which have been Christian. Foreign commerce, through the presence of the international business community, the training and technology brought to China, and the marketing of the goods themselves, has created a window through which Chinese can understand the outside world and the global community can understand China.

---

1. Lampton, *Following the Leader*, 37–38.
2. Towson and Woetzel, *1 Hour China* Book, chapter 3.
3. Ma, *The Chinese Exodus*, 15.

THE EMERGING URBAN CHURCH

China's wave of urbanization has seen the emergence of a vibrant Christian community in the cities. This urban revival is the result of several streams of believers who have together managed in various ways to utilize the changing cultural dynamics of the city to advance the Gospel.

During the 1970s and 1980s the church in the countryside experienced explosive growth as China embraced its open policy and loosened restrictions on religion. Driven by economic necessity, along with a desire to minister to their fellow migrants, many rural believers and, particularly, their children rode the wave of migration in the 1990s and 2000s and planted new churches in migrant communities. The "rural church in the city," as it is sometimes referred to, has struggled to adopt forms of worship and modes of ministry that are suited to this new generation and to the urban environment. Since many of these second-generation migrants will find themselves frustrated by a lack of educational and employment opportunities, particularly as China's manufacturing sector shrinks, the migrant church is being challenged to bring hope in practical ways to a generation facing a bleak future.

A second stream grew out of campus fellowships launched in the 1980s and 1990s as foreign teachers shared their faith and led many students to Christ. An urban pastor who traces his own spiritual roots back to the campus describes his early Christian experience:

> In those ten years, the Holy Spirit was moving. We knocked on dormitory doors and asked people, "Have you heard about the gospel? I want to share the gospel with you." Once, I talked with a guy for an hour. I used an evangelistic pamphlet and at the end asked if he wanted to make a prayer of decision. He said no. But someone sleeping in the bunk bed behind him popped up and said, "I do!" I said, "What? I didn't even know anyone was there!"
>
> . . . . After we graduated, we kept sharing the gospel in the marketplace and in our offices. We wanted to share our testimony with others, and the group of Christians that started in the university kept growing. . . . One brother had twenty people coming to his home for Bible studies. At this point he had never attended a church, only small groups. We did not know what we should do, or what would be next.[4]

This ambivalence hampered the development of campus fellowships, resulting in the need for "rechurching" Christians who had been trained

---

4. Wang, "China and the Church in China."

primarily in evangelism and whose Christianity was in many ways superficial. Their inability to establish contact with existing churches deprived them of the opportunity to learn from more experienced believers or to make the transition themselves into a local congregation.[5] The struggle of these fledgling churches revealed both the success and the shortcomings of English teaching ministry, which emphasized proclamation and, to some extent, discipleship, but which often left unanswered questions of ecclesiology.

A third stream comprises Christians returning from abroad. A significant number of Chinese who went overseas for study—some have estimated as high as ten percent—embraced Christianity. Among these are the generation that experienced the Tiananmen Massacre of 1989 and later left China, who saw perhaps the greatest turning to Christ among Chinese intellectuals in history. These disillusioned students and scholars shared a common pattern of having their hopes for their future and the future of their country dashed, seeking a new ideology to replace what they had lost, and meeting other Chinese who had gone through similar inner turmoil and eventually turned to Christ while overseas.[6] Lured by government incentives and business opportunities, many who became believers abroad have returned to China in the past two decades, where they participate in returnee fellowships and local churches.

These three streams all fall into the "unregistered" church category. Their congregations are not technically illegal, yet in the relatively open climate that has characterized China's cities since the 1990s they have faced minimal interference by authorities. A fourth stream comprises believers in the "registered" churches affiliated with the Three Self Patriotic Movement, the official organization charged with supervising the affairs of China's Protestant Christians under the guidance of the Communist Party. Although urban TSPM churches began reopening in the early 1980s and quickly became filled with worshipers on Sunday mornings, they catered mostly to older believers whose conversions dated back before the Cultural Revolution. In most cases children's programs were not permitted in these churches. Youth had little interest in exploring what was going on inside. In the decades since, many of these churches have undergone a transformation as younger pastors came into leadership and interest in the Gospel among young people grew.

---

5. Ma and Li, *Surviving the State, Remaking the Church*, 50–60.
6. Ma and Li, *Surviving the State, Remaking the Church*, 39.

WALKING WITH THE URBAN CHURCH

While thousands of pastors have been trained in the 20 Bible schools and seminaries operated under the auspices of the TSPM's sister organization, the China Christian Council, many times that number have been equipped in unofficial training institutions. Some leaders receive training in TSPM churches or officially sanctioned Bible schools but end up pastoring unregistered congregations. Many unregistered churches host their own training programs or even run small seminaries. In this area foreign workers, especially overseas Chinese pastors, have made a sizeable contribution through the provision of trainers, materials and funding.

During the decade of the 2000s, restrictions on activities for children and youth were loosened, with many urban churches offering full-fledged Sunday school programs and active youth groups. Training in children's ministry from foreign organizations and curricula provided by Hong Kong- or Taiwan-based ministries have contributed to this development in both the registered and unregistered church.

As China's urban Christians have sought to engage with their society in new ways, increased interaction with Christians from abroad has helped enlarge this space of activity and influence. Foreign Christian workers whose organizational ties or relationship networks spanned multiple cities or provinces have been able to make useful introductions among local Christians.

Sometimes Chinese believers from different traditions or networks find it difficult to come together due to a lack of trust and the perception that whoever calls the meeting must have an "agenda." By playing the role of neutral broker, a foreigner who has a relationship with both parties is able to create a safe space for interaction to occur. If things do not go as well as expected, the Chinese involved are less likely to lose face since it was the foreigner who called the meeting.

Foreign Christians have served as mentors to Chinese believers in emerging ministry areas such as publishing, counseling, social service and Christian education. They have provided training opportunities, funding, helpful overseas connections, and networking opportunities. In some cases the foreign worker has taken the lead in launching a new enterprise that then becomes a training ground for local believers, who eventually assume leadership. Through business arrangements some foreign workers have offered "cover" for fledgling entities that would have otherwise been unable to secure necessary legal permissions to operate openly.

CHANGING ROLES IN A CHANGING ENVIRONMENT

Today's foreign Christian workers are writing a new chapter in their China involvement. The changes in their role are motivated both by encouraging developments within China's church, as well as by sobering new political realities under President Xi Jinping's "New Normal." Understanding the multiple factors that are reshaping the context of Christian ministry in China is essential for organizations seeking to formulate a credible response.

Behind the changing role of foreign workers in China are at least four main drivers, two external to the ministry community and two internal. These combine to form the new environment in which foreign workers now operate.

A Maturing Church

In areas of church leadership, training, ministry formation, and even evangelism, much of what needed to be done by outsiders in the past is now being done by local believers. Where foreigners have been involved in church planting or leadership there now exists a need for local Christians to take the ministry to a new level. As mentioned earlier, the "growing pains" of the emerging urban church have been partly due to a lack of attention to ecclesiology among foreign workers. As Ma and Li explain:

> The problem of Christian believers whose lack of church fellowship has left them as orphans is exacerbated by the reality that most unregistered congregations in urban China stand alone and have minimal interaction with each other. Due to the lack of denominational structures, church leaders have not developed enough accountability. The traditional culture of "face-saving" comes in the way of conflict resolution and deters deeper communication between churches. Furthermore, the subculture of secrecy discourages efforts to collaborate.[7]

While foreign workers may have a future role in encouraging partnering among Chinese Christian leaders, it is ultimately up to these leaders to navigate their own future relationships and put in place indigenous structures for accountability and collaborative ministry.

---

7. Ma and Li, *Surviving the State, Remaking the Church*, 65.

The Policy Environment

China's 2016 Foreign NGO Law, revised religious regulations that went into effect in 2018, tightening visa restrictions, and a less hospitable business climate are all indicators of the larger policy shifts taking place under President Xi Jinping as he consolidates the Communist Party's grip on virtually every area of society. Xi's policies have been marked by a strong emphasis on national security and a concomitant mistrust of foreign organizations engaged in China. No longer valued for their technology and investments in China's business infrastructure, foreign companies are increasingly finding themselves sidelined. A rating system for foreigners puts a premium on advanced skills while making it more difficult for those with less training or experience—or those who have reached retirement age—to remain in China. With the National People's Congress decision in March 2018 to abolish term limits for China's president, the current trend shows little sign of abating any time soon.

Ian Johnson in his book *The Souls of China* relates the Party's increasing anti-foreign posture to its preference for "traditional" Chinese religions:

> [B]y early in the second decade of the twenty first century, the government's attitude toward traditional religion was shifting. From being viewed as superstition, or a cause of unrest, it was perceived as a source of morality and social cohesion for Chinese people and more acceptable than Protestant Christianity, with its foreign ties and interest in social change. Confucianism, on the other hand, offers an instant, made-in-China value system with a long track record of holding the country together.[8]

It is no surprise, therefore, that the involvement of foreign individuals and organizations and the promotion of Christian teaching from abroad are viewed as a threat. In a word, Christianity's foreign face causes the Party to lose face. Should this pressure intensify, urban church leaders will likely become increasingly circumspect in their foreign contacts and use of resources from abroad.

Internal Factors

The Western church viewed China as an urgent priority for ministry in the 1980s, but it has since lost its allure as a "closed country." Its rapid economic development has caused some to question whether China truly needs help

---

8. Johnson, *The Souls of China*, chapter 18.

from the West. Meanwhile, concern for the Muslim world has shifted much of the church's attention to the Middle East. The result has been a slowdown in new workers headed for China.

Meanwhile the sizeable generation of those who went to serve in China two or three decades ago is itself undergoing change, as family concerns, organizational transitions, and personal refocusing prompt more workers to leave China.

The internal changes will affect the foreign Christian community's response to the external ones. In what may appear to be an era of diminishing space for involvement and diminishing resources, much creativity is needed to discern the new opportunities inherent in this evolving environment.

IMPLICATIONS OF THE "NEW NORMAL"

The changing political climate presents new challenges both for Christians in China and for foreign workers who serve with them. As the Party moves from simply managing to "actively guiding" religion, local Christian leaders may be forced to make difficult choices regarding their relationship to the Party. Conflict will be inevitable as Chinese pastors respond in different ways, some choosing to espouse loyalty to the Party in order to continue their church ministry, and others taking a firm stand against working with the government. The resulting lack of unity could severely weaken the church, giving the Party leverage with which to turn believers against one another.

As the Chinese government endeavors to put religion "back in the box," Christian forays into areas such as publishing and education will likely be curtailed. As of this writing, it has already become extremely difficult to publish Christian content legally outside official church channels, whereas in past years commercial or academic presses had been willing to take on such projects provided outside funding was available. Education officials have stepped up actions against church-sponsored activities, including campus Bible studies, Christmas parties, and children's camps. While a dynamic Christian online community has blossomed in Chinese cyberspace over the past decade, the revised religion regulations that took effect in February 2018 specifically mention religious activity on the Internet, suggesting that this door of influence may begin closing at some point as well.

On the positive side, the current tightening under Xi Jinping has caused some local Christian leaders to rethink questions of church structure. Rather than continuing to pursue a mega church model—which may not be realistic should the government begin aggressively cracking down on standalone unregistered congregations—many are making plans to divide up into small groups, potentially extending the church's presence into new geographic areas.

Officially sanctioned churches under the TSPM are being pushed, in the name of "religion serving socialism," to do more in their communities. Meanwhile, the 2016 NGO law encourages the formation of local nonprofit organizations to address recognized social needs. While the law specifically restricts such organizations from engaging in religious activities, many Christians have nonetheless seized this opportunity to engage legally in serving their communities.

If they are unable to continue carving out separate "Christian" spaces within which to live out their faith, believers in both the official and unregistered church will be faced with the question of how to be "salt" within existing social structures. Christian-run local NGOs provide one example of how this can be done. Believers in the education, media and business fields will be pressed to find creative ways to present a Christian witness within environments that are becoming increasingly hostile to religion.

Finally, it is worth noting that persecution has, in the past, consistently served to strengthen the church in China. As China has urbanized and individual freedoms have increased over the past two decades, it has become much easier to be a Christian, or at least to be involved in Christian activities. Going to church has almost become fashionable in some quarters. Urban pastors complain of the "Sunday Christian" syndrome—of believers who seem eager to show up in church for worship yet whose lives during the week exhibit little evidence of a faith commitment. Should policies toward Christians continue to become more repressive, the church might well face another season of pruning, leading eventually to further growth.

For foreigners serving in China, the days of "coloring outside the lines" are over. When China first began opening up in the early 1980s there were few lines to speak of. It might have been possible to stay in China with one's family on a student visa for a decade, or to operate a business that never became profitable and had no customers, yet somehow managed to stay afloat. Today the government's heightened scrutiny of foreigners makes such ventures untenable.

Nor is it possible to successfully maintain one identity within China while presenting another to friends and supporting churches back home. Aided by advanced technology, China's security forces have become extremely efficient in "connecting the dots" in order to discern what foreigners are actually doing in China. To remain in China today requires a new type of integrity. A foreigner's story about their role and what they are actually doing must hang together both inside and outside China.

Assuming foreign workers are able to remain in country, they must carefully evaluate existing and future relationships with Chinese believers. Given growing anti-foreign sentiment, their presence may actually be a liability for local Christians. While local believers engaging in unauthorized religious activities may risk punishment by authorities, the risk increases exponentially when foreigners are involved. Foreign Christians and their local counterparts would be wise to have frank discussions about their respective tolerance for risk. They should formulate contingency plans to deal with situations that may arise as a result of their working together.

PASSING THE BATON

While most foreign Christian organizations active in China would agree their ultimate goal should be to work themselves out of a job, some have been more intentional than others in pursuing this goal. Especially in a season of relative openness, there is always more for the foreigners to do, and the need to turn over one's work to local believers and move on does not seem as urgent. While positive working relationships between foreigners and locals can be a great blessing to both sides, dependency upon foreign funds, leadership, methods or programs can stand in the way of the church's moving ahead toward independence and truly assuming ownership of the work. For foreign individuals and organizations, the security that comes with consistent support from concerned Christians back home, a predictable work environment, and the sense that one is truly "needed" in China mitigate against taking proactive efforts to develop local leadership and move on.

As the above survey of the current situation has shown, the realities facing foreign workers necessitate a new approach to serving in China. While a number of trends over time have contributed to bringing both the local church and foreign Christian community to this place, the pronounced political shift currently underway punctuates the significance of these trends with a profound sense of urgency.

The ChinaSource e-Book *Seven Trends Impacting Foreign Workers in China*[9] examines these in detail. Here we will focus on three paradigm shifts necessary for foreign Christian workers to effectively pass the baton and assume their new role.

---

9. China Source, "Seven Trends."

From Training to Mentoring

As mentioned above, training has long been a mainstay of service from the global church to the Chinese church. Offered within a variety of urban contexts, both form and informal, virtual and on-site, this basic biblical and theological training has served a critical need.

According to research by the China Gospel Research Alliance,[10] a consortium of China-focused organizations, Christian leaders in China anticipate that, in the future the need for training from outside China will fall in proportion to the need for mentoring. Several factors account for this anticipated shift:

1. The education level among believers, particularly in the cities, has risen significantly. There are more Chinese believers who have received advanced theological training by going abroad and who are now back in China and available to train others.

2. Advances in technology and the availability of urban infrastructure and resources have helped spawn a host of training options now available in country, including networks of unregistered schools, online offerings from overseas, and the approximately 20 seminaries and Bible schools operating under the auspices of the China Christian Council, many of which offer extension programs through churches around the country.

3. While urban believers today may be more likely to have received the training required for basic church ministries, many are now pioneering new areas of service and outreach. These specialized areas include consulting, family ministry, youth ministry, and service to disadvantaged segments of society. In addition to knowledge specific to these sectors, those who are on the cutting edge of local Christian NGO work also need training in non-profit management and fund raising. Thus the need for specialized equipping by those with experience in these areas. This mentoring is best done one-to-one or in small groups rather than in a classroom setting.

4. Although formal ministry training has imparted knowledge and skills, it has often come up short in addressing leaders' personal life issues. These include roadblocks in relationships, family life, and spiritual growth. Foreign workers who understand the context and who have relationships with these leaders can serve as mentors, walking with them as they address these critical areas.

10. Fulton, "Journeying with the Church in China."

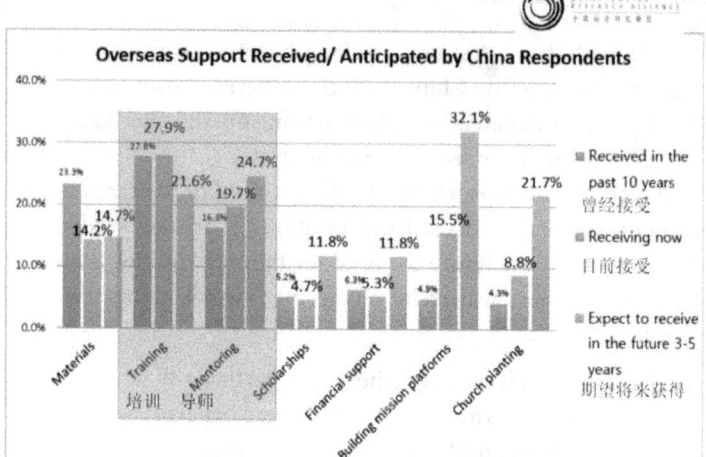

Writing in the spring 2017 issue of *ChinaSource Quarterly*, Steve Z, a Chinese Christian from a house church background, makes the case for mentoring:

> Simply introducing courses from overseas will impact how the Chinese church develops. However, for the Chinese preachers who have received training from the West and Chinese seminaries overseas, the challenges they encounter in their ministries cannot be resolved in ways based upon their predecessors' experiences. Quite naturally, they seek help and wisdom from the overseas resources that are familiar to them. This is the primary reason that Chinese Christian preachers long for the company of a mature and experienced pastor from overseas. The question is, however, are the pastoral colleagues overseas prepared to deal with their issues? Are they willing to be humble, to devote themselves to understanding all the issues the Chinese churches encounter including: societal, and economical, as well as the unique cultural and theological implications?[11]

As Steve points out, the current need of China's Christian leaders raises the bar significantly for those who would go to China to serve them. It also raises the question of how Christians outside China will rise to meet this challenge.

---

11. Stephen Z., "The Expectations of the Chinese Church."

From Solutions to Shared Innovation

In his classic volume, *To Change China*, historian Jonathan Spence documents the stories of various foreigners who came to China in past centuries. Among these were missionaries, engineers, merchants, and doctors. They all dedicated their lives to addressing what they saw as critical needs or opportunities. While all believed they were bringing lasting change to China, in the end it was they themselves who were changed, and not China.

Foreigners living long-term in China are by necessity resourceful. Like the real-life characters in Spence's book, they see themselves as agents of change. The challenges they encounter are an invitation to exercise their ingenuity and devise solutions. If something needs fixing, they'll find a way.

This ingenuity may have been an asset to foreign Christian workers in China over the past three-and-a-half decades. In the current situation it could become a liability. While the church of a generation ago welcomed many "teachers" from abroad, the urban Chinese church of today is increasingly well educated, cosmopolitan in its outlook, forward-thinking, and creative.

Foreign workers who still assume their role is to come up with solutions on behalf of believers in China may actually become part of the problem. In the current environment, their local counterparts will often see the challenges in ways the foreigner cannot understand. They will likely introduce new options that, while outside the foreigner's frame of reference, make perfect sense in the Chinese context.

The opportunity here is for shared innovation. Both parties bring something of value to the table. Together they can find a way forward that will ultimately be more effective than if either side approached the problem alone.

One recent example has been the creative way in which Chinese Christians utilize social media. China's WeChat is miles ahead of other platforms being developed elsewhere in the world. More than a messaging platform, it comprises an entire online environment. Chinese netizens transacting many of their daily activities within this environment may see little need for the traditional Internet.

Foreign content providers who have focused on traditional platforms and on strategies to get around China's "Great Firewall" in order to avoid possible censorship have missed the genius of WeChat. Some may have invested needlessly in systems that ultimately proved ineffective. Those who teamed up with local Christians who are innovating within China's thriving online Christian community, on the other hand, ended up with a product that is much more "Chinese" and thus more likely to make a meaningful and lasting contribution.

Confucius is purported to have said to his disciples, "In a company of three, one is my teacher." This proverb is an appropriate reminder that we all, Chinese and non-Chinese, have much to learn from one another. Now more than ever, those who seek to make a difference in China would do well to discover the teachers in their midst.

From Sending to Receiving

The effort among international faith-based organizations to get to China began in earnest in the late 1980s. As they opened up and developed, China's cities provided the natural gateway for foreign workers to come and play a role. As a result, tens of thousands headed to China in the succeeding decades.

Now it is China's turn. Building upon a vision for missions that first emerged as the "Back to Jerusalem" movement early in the last century and was subsequently rekindled in the late 1990s, China's church is now preparing to send workers from China to the nations. Greater personal freedoms, more financial resources within the church, increased global awareness, and growing business opportunities abroad provide the impetus for this movement. In response, international faith-based organizations are considering how to receive these workers as they venture to foreign lands.

In the China Gospel Research Alliance survey referred to above, Chinese Christian leaders and leaders of foreign organizations engaged in China were asked what kind of support churches in China will need most in the future. Both agreed that a key area will be building mission platforms. They also agreed that the Chinese church's greatest future contribution to the global church would be in the area of missions. Yet only 20 percent of foreign and overseas Chinese respondents viewed assisting the Chinese church in this area as a priority, compared to 69 percent of China respondents.[12]

Both sides need to be prepared to assume new roles. Many caution that the Chinese church still lacks sufficient infrastructure, experience, training, and grassroots support. Most believers are Han Chinese who have had little if any prolonged exposure to cultures other than their own. Church leaders talk excitedly about missions, yet the track record of individual congregations sending and supporting workers overseas has not been encouraging.

International organizations welcome the prospect of new workers coming from China. Yet foreign workers who have served long-term

---

12. Fulton, "Journeying with the Church in China."

in China warn against ignoring ongoing needs within the church such as training, mentoring, and discipleship. If the church in China is going to engage effectively in sustained cross-cultural outreach, they point out, then these needs must be addressed.

Writing in the 2016 winter issue of *ChinaSource Quarterly*, guest editor Wu Xi cautioned international organizations against recreating colonial structures by viewing China as a recruitment ground:

> Hoisting an outside agency's flag will not help China build its own mission program unless an explicit agreement is reached to train such aspiring missionaries for a specific period of time and then release them back to their own church or sending structure in China. What China does not need is a structure of branch offices of outside agencies similar to the way Western denominations organized as they carved up China as a mission field before the 1940s. What China does need is to develop its own mission leaders so they can build mission structures that can be owned by the Chinese church.[13]

While the transition from sending to receiving has begun, this transition must be negotiated carefully for the sake of the Chinese church's long-term role in fulfilling its global mission.

RIDING THE WAVES OF CHANGE

Emerging from the chaos of the Cultural Revolution in the 1970s, China experienced a rural revival that spread like wildfire across the countryside. In the 1990s, with urbanization beginning to forever transform the landscape of China, God brought a wave of workers from abroad who helped nurture a new kind of church in the cities, creating a movement that is now at the forefront of Chinese Christianity. Once the evangelists, church planters, and entrepreneurs responsible for new urban ministry initiatives, foreign workers today no longer function as the trailblazers or pioneers, Instead, they find themselves drawn in new directions as China assumes prominence on the world scene and as China's church prepares to go global. As their focus shifts from serving China and its church to serving *with* the church in China, new roles and opportunities await those who are willing to ride the waves of change.

---

13. Xi and TT, "China Emerging."

Chapter 2

Foreign Business Leaders Using Kingdom Values to Transform the Workplace

Elisabeth Kim

CURRENT NEEDS IN CHINA FOR MISSIONARIES/ TENTMAKERS IN THE WORKPLACE

> [14] You are the light of the world. A town built on a hill cannot be hidden. [15] Neither do people light a lamp and put it under a bowl. Instead they put it on its stand, and it gives light to everyone in the house. [16] In the same way, let your light shine before others, that they may see your good deeds and glorify your Father in heaven (Matthew 5:14–16).

I have seen many foreign business leaders represent Christ in their respective offices, in times of flourishing and in times of difficulty. This has been one of the best examples to the Chinese locals of the biblical way to live out their faith. It provides contextual evidence and clear application, which otherwise is not preached from the pulpit or provided case studies.

The presence of tentmakers also helps local Chinese to recognize the need to not compartmentalize their work and faith. It is often easy to get lost in work and not integrate the Sunday learnings into the Monday through

Friday. Dare I say that the majority of discipleship actually can and should happen in the office. The Chinese professional sphere is often more demanding, time-consuming, and lacks boundaries comparatively to the Western professional expectations. This also lends itself to the lack of male attendance in the church, especially participation in small groups during the weekdays, because males are expected to be climbing the socioeconomic ladder. When there are strong examples of well-respected business leaders, especially male, living out their faith in challenging situations, this sets up young professionals to consider how they too are called to live out their faith as well.

Women in the Workplace

The workforce in China is currently feeling the pressures and stresses of trying to maintain a balance between their fast-paced urban lifestyle and a career of significance. This growing pressure has become more evident in the increasing number of millennials in the workforce. Millennials represent the single largest generational group in the Chinese workforce at 30 percent. As a result of the pressure and lack of leadership at the workplace, employee retention is noted to be low. Another significant change in the Chinese workforce is that the number of women in the urban workforce is growing and they play a key role in China's growing business world.

Women in the workforce, specifically the millennials, are facing new challenges with the choices they have that were "unavailable" to their predecessors. The women desire a more holistic direction in life and their work, as well as higher expectations in their career development and career path. Recent data indicates a turnover rate of 26 percent among female millennials in China. With 43 million enterprises and a 50 billion dollar human resources industry, companies need to identify and invest in their rising female leaders in order to retain them.

Research indicates that emphasizing/featuring successful female role models dramatically increases the number of women leaders in the workforce. Our goal is to shift women's perceptions of what they can accomplish as the first step in bringing gender equity to the industry.

Case Study: Light in Darkness

Daniel was a director in a large city in China of a large multi-national organization. He was well respected among the Chinese community and even by governing officials. Around his fifth year, a very difficult General Manager took over the leadership position within the office. He created a very toxic work environment, and many in the office suffered. Daniel wondered whether or not he should quit and felt depressed. It was at this time, he clung to the Lord and pressed in. He chose not to join the complaining bitter spirit of other co-workers, and would encourage his co-workers and his own employees. They witnessed how he suffered the most and shielded his team, but similar to the prophet Isaiah, did not open his mouth to retort to the GM. Soon, a few of them asked him how he was able to do it. This was the first time he was able to share the gospel with many in the office, as well as show the local Chinese believers in the office how a Christian can respond to suffering in the workplace. A Bible study started and continues to this day.

Takeaway:

The gospel come out best in the context of suffering. The local church often does not teach practical ways to deal with suffering in the workplace. This is especially true in China, as the workforce is in its developmental stages. Many difficult situations arise especially around difficult management, as leaders who are skilled in technical work lack the leadership know-how as we see in the states. The majority of Chinese millennials dislike their jobs and many of them do not have a way out. Foreign business leaders in China have a huge opportunity to completely change the culture in their teams. Many would feel the impact and be open for conversations around values. Many Chinese who are in suffering situations will be more open to having conversations around purpose in faith.

Case Study: Prayer and Confirmation

Emily was the CMO of a Fortune 40 company in a large Chinese city on the east coast. Many women in the office knew of her faith, but she wasn't able to explicitly share. She had asked God if she was meant to stay, and asked for confirmation. That next morning she met another Christian, Jess, at the coffee station. She started praying with that sister over the office spiritual climate. Jess read Joshua and felt personally led to prayer walk around the office seven times, and encountered a few seekers during that walk. Soon, the two of them started meeting seekers in the workplace. They individually were able to share and minister and saw two of the seekers come to faith.

Takeaway: Passing on the Power of Prayer

Many local Chinese have not experienced prayer in and for the workplace. One of the most powerful things we can pass on as believers is the power of prayer to transform the physical space, to takedown strongholds. As we see in Joshua 8, in order of the walls of Jericho to fall, Joshua and the Israelites needed to walk around the city in faith and obedience for the walls to fall down. In the same way, before beginning any ministry or reaching out to people, the most powerful way we can partner with God and encourage local believers is to pray over their workspaces, their co-workers and managers, to break down any spiritual strongholds from the enemy.

Case Study: Daring to Disciple

Darren was a director of a large pharmaceutical company in China. He prayed for a younger Christian brother to come in to help him initiate conversations with co-workers as it was difficult due to his status in the company. Matt ended up joining the company as a senior manager. Together they started a Bible study during lunch in a cafe below the office. Other believers started joining. As many of these co-workers traveled on weekends due to sales positions, they had not joined a local church or small group. Many of them also did not know that community was an essential part of the Christian walk, as they came to faith in the U.S. These lunch Bible studies were extremely effective as they were able to share and pray, getting closer as a team.

How Chinese Churches can be Prepared to Minister to the Chinese Business Sector

We have seen two major types of Chinese believers in the business sector who have transformative potential:

- White Collar Professionals: Chinese post-college professionals ages 23–30 who are currently active in a local Chinese church but facing challenges in their current workplace situation
- Senior Business leaders: these are the Chinese in senior positions, often too busy to have time for community or church

How do we empower White Collar Professionals?

Context

The Chinese house church separates the secular and the sacred from their teaching and because of this there is a huge need to integrate training, holistic teaching, case studies, and helpful content that is targeted to the younger generation. There is a huge danger of becoming irrelevant to the Gen Z Chinese young people in the urban cities if the gospel is not shared and taught in a relevant way through their mediums.

We need to compete for the eyes, ears, and hearts of the young professionals who struggle with feeling disconnected in the workplace, lack mentors, and desire meaning and purpose in their work. All of these topics have such strong answers in the gospel. The church is just under-equipped to tell them.

Recommendation

1. Partner with local Chinese churches to equip young professionals to live out their faith in the workplace by establishing an annual one-day summit to bring Christian millennials together.
2. Establish cohort groups (12–20 individuals) to provide monthly accountability and a "safe" environment for discussion about challenges, growth, fellowship, and prayer.
3. Leadership training will provide new/additional skill sets which will benefit employers, the church, and the participant. Mentorship through the cohort groups will provide meaningful connection and networking, and allow for personal relationships to be established.
4. Leadership development topics and/or monthly cohort group meetings can include topics such as: prayer in the workplace, purpose and calling, family and work priorities, and real ethics and scripture.
5. The cohort group will be responsible for planning the next annual summit. This will provide tangible workplace experience and skills for the cohort members.
6. For cohort groups the goal is to multiply and reach additional professionals in the coming years. Cohort members will be expected to recruit new professionals to join as cohort members in future years.

How do we empower Senior Business leaders?

Context

Senior business leaders' responsibilities and lives are so overtaken by demands and travel of the workplace. They are also in a season of life where demands from family are ramping up quickly. The opportunity to serve in the local church often is limited to things like Sunday school or worship, which also takes directly away from their time, but also does not utilize their skillset and amazing management/leadership skills. However, pastors often don't have time to think about this subset of their congregation and often just label them as too busy/self-important to truly contribute to the church. Pastors need to be shown a different way of engaging with this really important and unique group of members.

Recommendation

1. Create small groups of senior leaders to pray and intercede for one another. CEO groups are one of the most effective ways for them to not only network but identify with each other and mentor one another in areas of struggles and having like-minded encouragement.
2. Provide Business as Mission opportunities where leaders can leverage their high travelling demands to include speaking engagements or mentorship opportunities with local bodies in the areas they have to travel to.
3. Business Ethics conferences and summits provide tangible ways for Senior Business Leaders to contribute where their God-given giftings and passions are. In a time when the security is getting tighter, there is an amazing opportunity to have kingdom minded leaders share their faith and character lessons with both nonbelievers and believers alike.
4. Ensure more broader teaching and training, as well as opportunities for local senior leaders to engage with Western senior business leaders both from a mentorship opportunity, networking opportunity, and also to brainstorm of ways to combine the kingdom and business. As the world is getting more and more global, this is an amazing way for practical learning and real stories to reach this hard-to-reach population.

5. Translated work and faith books are great tools for this cohort: *The Great Endeavor* by Tim Keller; *The Circle Maker* by Mark Batterson; and, Global Leadership Summit CDs as well.

6. Christian Career and Life Coaches are an amazing partner to bring into these rising leaders as it benefits both their business lives as well as spiritual lives. Definitely being selective of the right kingdom-minded ones is very key. Amazing career and life coaches are able to frame new objectives and mindsets for the Chinese leaders to envision a new way of working, a new way of thinking about their people, and a new way of seeing themselves.

All in all, please pray for this growing urban population of Chinese believers. They really are the ones to carry the torch of the gospel throughout their companies and God-willing, westward. Please pray that He sends more harvest workers to the field, more disciple-makers that inspire more to become disciple-makers.

Chapter 3

Reaching Educated Chinese through Teaching English

TABOR LAUGHLIN

This chapter relates to an outreach need in China that is particularly for missionaries from English speaking countries. A phenomenon prevalent in all corners of China is the opportunity to teach English full-time in local Chinese schools. One can teach to many different levels or varying ages of students, including teaching little kids at a private English school, teaching middle school or high school students, or teaching English within a college setting. Opportunities to do this are immense. Generally speaking, these jobs are not even close to forty hours per week jobs, so these English teaching jobs allow for lots of other time to do ministry and to learn Chinese. Usually native English speakers only need a bachelor's degree to teach English, but not necessarily a degree or background in TESOL or English or education. My degree was in engineering and I had no prior experience, but the university I started at in eastern China hired me right out of college to teach English there. My wife's major in college was finance, but she also got hired right out of college to teach English. A native English speaker often just needs a bachelor's degree of any kind to teach English in China. Also, there are English teaching opportunities for native English speakers of all ages, from just out of college, all the way up to sixty-five years old or so.

A good question is if there really are that many opportunities in China to teach English. For the last few decades, the Chinese government has encouraged students to learn English as their second language. Most children now start learning English when they're in elementary school or earlier. Usually it is Chinese teachers that teach the kids a basic knowledge of English writing, reading and vocabulary. Native English speakers can best help the Chinese students speak the language in a more authentic and native way. Many schools in China now are hiring foreigners to teach English. The huge Chinese population combined with large numbers of that population learning English, results in many English teaching jobs being available for native English speakers. My contacts at schools in China are regularly telling me they need help finding more foreign English teachers. There is an abundance of spoken English teaching openings in schools around China. The main thing lacking is not these kinds of job openings, but rather having enough native English speakers to fill the teaching spots there. The missionary could help by filling these open positions.

There are many perks to teaching English in China. As previously mentioned, the schools often provide free housing at the school and a reasonable salary. Living on the campus opens up opportunities to minister either to students there, or to Chinese teachers and their families who also live at the school. The salary from the school is plenty for a single person to live off, or even for a married couple. In my ten years in China, I was always an English teacher, usually within a university setting. At first I did this as a single guy, then being married, and eventually having a daughter there. In my ten years of living in China, I never had to raise financial support. After I got married, my wife also had some income through teaching part- or full-time. The pay from the school has always been enough for me as a single guy and for us as a small family. I think about the many missionaries in China who raise tens of thousands of dollars each year to serve in China. For some people—like myself—it can be a good option to teach in China and get paid, instead of having to raise money to be serving in China.

Another big plus for this teaching job is that the school not only gives us a salary and a free apartment, but they give us a work visa. This means that we can legally live there for the entire year or longer. We can renew it each year in our city in China without having to leave China. There are so many missionaries who do not have jobs and end up living long-term in China on tourist visas. In this situation, the families would leave the country every few months to renew their visas. It seems to me, that for many people, having a work visa can be much less stressful, and there is no need to constantly be spending money each year to leave the country to renew a tourist or other shorter-term visas.

Our jobs as English teachers are not just so we can get a visa. Even more importantly is that our teaching jobs give us a significant place in the Chinese society. Chinese people greatly value education. So the Chinese people around us respect us, because we are helping their kids learn English and do better as students. Some missionaries in China have not had legitimate jobs and thus the Chinese are suspicious of them. These missionaries have often struggled to answer these questions from Chinese: "What are you doing here?" "Why are you here?" "Since you have no job here, where does all your money come from?"

But for teachers like us, the Chinese do not look at us with suspicion; rather, they look at us with trust and appreciation. When people trust us and appreciate our contribution to the Chinese society, then they are more likely to be open to hearing the gospel from us because there is a level of trust already built up between us. The English teaching jobs provide an inlet into the Chinese society and help us to be contributing members of the Chinese community around us. This job may allow more open doors to make close friends with those we work with or those we teach.

TEACHING IN A UNIVERSITY

Teaching English at a Chinese university opens up unique doors for ministry. Usually the weekly class load is between fifteen to twenty hours of class a week. Chinese universities are great places for ministry for several reasons. The school usually provides free housing on campus for the foreign teachers. This means that college students can easily come to your place and hang out with you. There are Chinese college students all around you, so if you make any effort at all, you can relatively quickly make some good Chinese friends, either through the classes you teach, or through going to English Corners on campus, or just by doing things like playing basketball with them outside on the basketball courts.

Chinese college students are at a prime time for being ministered to. Firstly, being around college age is when many people around the world move away from their homes for the first time and often can begin to be open to learn new things and try to get a better understanding of the world. Chinese college students are curious and they want to learn about the world. Many of them really want to improve their English. They're interested in learning about foreign cultures and Western cultures. They like to have Western friends. These Chinese college students are incredibly welcoming to us as Westerners, and particularly those foreigners coming from English speaking countries.

Chinese college students are not only curious to learn about the world, but often when they are in college, it is the first time they are able to have any kind of free time in their lives and can organize their own time. For most Chinese students, from their early years in elementary school all the way through high school, their lives consist of being at school and doing homework. High school is the most intense years of their lives, as they prepare night and day for the college entrance exam. Each student is trying to get into a good college. Once they make it to college, they suddenly have lots of free time. For missionaries who are English teachers in Chinese high schools or middle schools, the students are too busy to spend time with their English teacher during these years as they are the testing years for the students. They do homework and are at class nearly constantly. So this situation leads to limitations for ministry for the missionary to the younger student. But for Chinese college students, they have free time to spend with the missionary and are at a point in their lives when they are exploring and curious. It is easy for one to meet the students to eat in the school cafeteria or at a restaurant off-campus. A teacher can play sports, go shopping together, explore the city, or take a walk at a park with students during free time. During holidays, an English teacher may be able to go home with a student to that student's hometown to see their home and family. There are many opportunities for a university teacher to develop deep relationships with a university student. Through this tight bond, a university teacher can be used to slowly direct a student towards knowing Jesus.

HOW THIS MINISTRY IS CONNECTED WITH LOCAL HOUSE CHURCHES

Can missionaries teaching English actually work together with local house church believers? What is the suggested extent to which local believers and foreign missionary English teachers cooperate? In my experience, I found that my role as an English teacher in China was not to directly plant new house churches. Rather, the best tactic for ministry for me was to work closely with a local house church and the leaders within it. My role was to do evangelism with the students or Chinese teachers at the school. When someone was interested in the gospel, my task was not to lead that person in planting a church, nor to lead the church myself. What I saw as a longer-lasting tactic was for those from the school who come to faith to be introduced to the local house church. I became a networker instead of a church planter. Hopefully, the students get connected with the local house church and eventually become an active member of the house church. This led to a better result than me starting a house church on my own from the school where I taught. This didn't mean that I cut off all contact with student friends who were introduced to the local church. I still needed to care for them and reach out to them. There may be a need for me to continue to disciple that person. I could encourage that person to get plugged into a local church. This is a way I found to pass on this ministry to the local house churches, as they ideally will remain in the house church when I might be gone.

On the topic of student ministry and passing the students on to others, I found that just because a Chinese student (or another person) makes a profession of faith, doesn't mean they will automatically persevere in the faith long-term. Lots of times they may be interested in Christianity because they wanted a Western friend. The student wanted to please me because they knew I wanted them to know Jesus. And if the main communication with that person outside class was in English, then the student may be attracted to the idea of getting more opportunities to develop their English ability with a native speaker. When a Chinese person is interested in the Bible or makes a profession of faith, certainly I would rejoice; however, I didn't know that person's deeper motives. Even if their motives at first were bad and for their own selfish gain rather than any real curiosity in the faith, maybe the Lord will change their bad motives into pure motives.

How can an English teacher pass on the ministry of these students when they graduate and move to another city to work? Of course the teacher needs to continue to keep in touch with the student and encourage them towards joining a local house church in their new city. Oftentimes I have seen Chinese students really flounder when they move away and need to find a local house church in that new city. This reveals an even greater importance in introducing students to local house churches while they're still at college. Then they can become comfortable worshipping with other local believers and become comfortable worshiping in Chinese. This way, when they graduate and move to another city to work, they will have more urgency to find a solid house church near them and to get involved. But if they have not connected with a local house church while in college and their only experiences of reading the Bible or praying have been in English with foreigners, once they move to another city upon graduation it will be hard for them to plug into a local house church. They may think it strange to try to sing worship songs, read the Bible, and pray in Chinese. And they may have little motivation to find a local Chinese house church there. This again underscores the need to introduce them to a local house church as soon as possible.

A final way that doing outreach through teaching language relates to the Chinese house churches is the reality of Chinese missionaries being sent to foreign countries to minister. We as native English speakers can move to many countries around the world to teach English. As already mentioned in this chapter, we can get a visa, a salary, and an immediate connection to locals there. We can contribute to the local community in that area. In the same way, Chinese believers who are sent as missionaries to certain countries may also have opportunities to do missions through teaching Chinese. In the same way, they can get a work visa, a steady salary, and have a significant role in the local community and immediate people around them to become friends with.

CONCLUSION

At this point in history, God has opened a huge door in China for ambassadors of the gospel to come as English teachers from English speaking countries. China historically has not always been so open to having Westerners go and live there. In fact, there have been many centuries in China's history in which the rulers were strongly opposed and antagonistic to having any outsiders or Westerners living in their country. Most recently this antagonism existed during Chairman Mao's reign, and China was completely closed to most of the rest of the world. Many Chinese dynasties historically have been closed to any interaction with Westerners. And no one knows down the road how long China's great demand for learning English will continue. But at least for this period of time, English is the international language, and China is developing economically and trying to be an economic power. China understands how critical the English language is to their current and future success. Praise God for these developments over the past few decades. And may many English speakers from around the world answer the call to use the English language for the purpose of ministry to the Chinese.

PART II

Social Impact on Chinese Society

Chapter 4

Bioethics, Abortion and Missions in China

John Ensor

Winston Churchill said of Russia, "It's a riddle wrapped in a mystery inside an enigma." I have long felt this a better description of China. The only accurate way to describe China is to say, "It's complex." Its long history, ethnic peoples, languages, religions, politics, education system, even the organization of the Church—underground (unregistered) networks along with the government approved churches—and the degree of compliance or defiance they exhibit along with the ever-changing restrictions, threats and arrests, they experience, means that everything about China is challenging relative to the global cause of Christ.

To these challenges, I want to add another great challenge: bioethics. John Kilner, the Professor of Bioethics and Contemporary Culture at Trinity International University provides a workable introduction: "Bioethical challenges have to do with life and health ('bio'), and what one does about them should flow from wise discernment about what is good and right ('ethics')."[1] In contemporary culture, the bioethical discernment needed most revolves around abortion. Bioethics covers more, (cloning, artificial reproductive technologies, and the like), but abortion is the one immediate challenge that is ever-present, having already touched every family, church, and people group worldwide, altering marriage, family and the culture at large. By extension, the way we respond to abortion has ramifications that

---

1. Kilner, *Why The Church Needs Bioethics*, 11.

fling outwardly into the culture, from the sanctity of marriage to human trafficking to physician assisted suicide.

In my world, we speak of a*pplied* bioethics. Here the emphasis is on the practical good works that flow from a biblical view of human value. To mention just a few examples, the Christian view of human value lead to the practical work of the underground railroad in the USA. It put an end to widow burning (sati or suttee) in India, twin-killing in Africa, and foot-binding in China. It created innumerable ministries to the orphan, the alcoholic, the prostitute, the mentally ill, the blind, refugees fleeing war and immigrants fleeing poverty.[2] Why? Because our fellow man is *more valuable* than many sparrows.

Applied bioethics refers to how being for life (prolife) in theological conviction leads to the good works of rescuing (Pr 24:10–12), defending (Ps 82:3–4), speaking up (Pr 31:8–9), and intervening just as Jesus pointed to the life-saving actions of the Samaritan and said, "Go and do likewise" (Lk 10:37).

Answering God's call to cherish and defend innocent human life from being unjustly killed is valid in and of itself. Yet what I have learned over the past thirty years is that prolife work, more specifically, the work of *pregnancy crisis intervention and after-abortion care*, is proving to be a major entry point for engaging secular culture and closed religions with the gospel.

PREGNANCY HELP ORGANIZATIONS (PHO) ARE THE NEW MEDICAL MISSIONS

Around the world, most of this engagement happens through the development of pregnancy help organizations (PHOs). According to the Lozier Institute, "The first free-standing pregnancy center in North America opened its doors in 1968 in Toronto, Canada, under the name of Birthright. Thus began a distinct, new 'service arm' of the pro-life movement, offering compassion and practical assistance to women facing unexpected or unwelcomed pregnancies."[3]

In the last fifty years, over 5,300 pregnancy help organizations have been set up by Christians, with half of these *outside* the USA. The database kept by Heartbeat International, as of this writing, lists 571 PHOs in South

---

2. For more, see Alvin Schmidt's excellent book, *How Christianity Changed the World* (Grand Rapids: Zondervan 2004).

3. Charlotte Lozier Institute. "A Half Century of Hope"

America, 483 in Africa, ninety-eight in Asia, 1,420 in Europe and eighty-one in Australia.[4]

In China, the model emerging for PHOs are counseling offices opening within the OBGYN department of hospitals. They are also using various strategies like a national hotline and the messaging app WeChat to connect with women or couples in pregnancy crisis. These efforts serve both secular Han Chinese women and couples in pregnancy crisis, along with Uighur Muslims, Tibetan Buddhists and many others. Several safe homes for unmarried mothers have also opened. The most recent home was set up by unregistered house churches working together, across networks, staffed and supported by local donations.

In the past, setting up medical clinics and hospitals provided an instant entry point into people's lives. No matter their religion, world-view, or language, everybody got sick. When they did, the crisis of pain and the threat of death opened them up to Christians and their medical care. With every single patient, and by extension their social circle, Christian medical care transmitted the Christian view of human value upon which the gospel is based. Today, that is happening again in the world of pregnancy crisis intervention.

Understanding the mission field created by abortion[5]

> Some years ago, my phone rang. The caller's voice quivered as she told me she was sixteen years old. Her emotions were so intense that she spoke haltingly, *"If I don't get . . . an abortion . . . I'm going to kill myself."* Before I could respond, she revealed her full anguish. *"But I know after my abortion, I won't be able to live with what I've done. . . . I will need to kill myself."* "

This teenager was experiencing crisis—a pregnancy-related crisis. More particularly, she was experiencing a crisis of *faith* and a search for *salvation*.

Abortion is *always* a crisis of *faith*. As John Piper says, "Abortion is about God."[6] It is what people do instead of looking to God for help and

---

4. Data based on Heartbeat International's database as of Spring 2018.

5. This phrase was coined by Kurt Dillinger, President of Life International (lifeinternational.org). In personal correspondence to the author, Dillinger writes, "As a missions pastor in the late 90s, I spoke of the global mission field created by abortion as I came to recognize the pre-born as a people group, a hidden people group, a persecuted people group and an unreached people group."

6. See John Piper, "Where Does Child-Killing Come From?" Sermon, from January 25, 1998. https://www.desiringgod.org/messages/where-does-child-killing-come-from

satisfaction. His comments are based on James 4:2, "You want something but don't have it, so you kill. You don't have it because you do not ask God." Abortion is a substitute for prayer.

Strange and perverse as their end is, abortionists parrot the same message that Christ offers to those in trouble: "Come to me, all who labor and are heavy laden, and I will give you rest. Take my yoke upon you. . .and find rest for your souls" (Mt 11:28–29). Abortionists promise salvation and rest too. But they require a very different kind of yoke—death and the spiritual death that flows from the bloodguilt of shedding innocent blood.

My caller was frightened and desperate. Her pregnancy felt like death—the end of her life. True, her pregnancy was not a fatal disease, but it did present a mortal threat to her life *as she had projected it*. Getting an abortion was, in her mind, a life-saving necessity.

At the same time, my caller expected that abortion, while resolving one crisis, would create another. Her extreme language was her way of expressing what lies at the heart of a pregnancy-related crisis: the humanity of the unborn.

As Apologist, Scott Klusendorf writes,

"The science of embryology tells us that from the earliest stages of development, the unborn are distinct, living, and whole human beings. Leading embryology books confirm this. For example, Keith L. Moore & T.V.N. Persaud write, "A zygote is the beginning of a new human being. Human development begins at fertilization, the process during which a male gamete or sperm. . .unites with a female gamete or oocyte. . .to form a single cell called a zygote. This highly specialized, totipotent cell marks the beginning of each of us as a unique individual."[7]

Either by moral education or by a natural connection to motherhood, my caller understood why abortion is morally wrong. It is the intentional killing of an innocent human being. Aborting her unborn child presented itself as something wholly contrary to her self-image and pride in being a caring person. Her contemplation of suicide subsequent to her abortion was in anticipation of not being able to live with the subsequent guilt and grief.

This young woman's life was about to change. Crisis always produces change. Whether she would change in healthy and redemptive ways or whether she would change in wounding and alienating ways was yet unknown to me. But one thing is sure; she is not alone.

Based on abortion rates worldwide, it is probable that more people around the world experience crisis from unexpected pregnancy *than any*

---

7. Klusendorf, "Defending Your Prolife Views," 8–11.

other event. The Alan Guttmacher Institute, a leading research organization committed to abortion advocacy worldwide, report the following:

- During 2010–14, an estimated 56 million induced abortions occurred each year worldwide. This number represents an increase from 50 million annually during 1990–94, mainly because of population growth.
- Globally, 25 percent of pregnancies ended in abortion in 2010–14. In developed countries, the proportion declined from 39 percent to 28 percent between 1990–94 and 2010–14, whereas it increased from 21 percent to 24 percent in developing countries.[8]

On the other hand, Robert S. Johnston has shown that Guttmachers estimate of 56 million is almost all guess-work and that they have reasons for always estimating high. Johnsons research shows that actual reported abortions worldwide are around 11.5 million. But since many countries don't report, this figure represents a base number.

Further, according to the medical journal, *The Lancet*, world-wide abortion data indicates that abortion is especially concentrated in three regions of the world: Asia, East Europe and the Caribbean.[9]

ABORTION, INFANTICIDE AND GENDERCIDE IN CHINA

The highest number of abortions in the world are in China. China's National Health Population and Family Planning Commission reports that 13 million women annually terminate unplanned pregnancies. But official news media outlets also reported at least an additional 10 million chemically induced abortions are performed in nongovernment facilities.

Reggie Littlejohn notes, "The population of the United States is about 320 million, with about 1 million abortions per year. The population of China is almost 1.4 billion, with about 23 million abortions per year. Therefore, with four times the population of the United States, China has 23 times the number of abortions."

Abortion in China has been driven to extremes by the population control measures adopted in China in 1979 and known as the *One Child Policy (OCP)*.[10]

8. Guttmacher Institute. "Induced Abortion Worldwide."
9. See Sedgh, G., et al., "Abortion Incidence between 1990 and 2014: Global, Regional, and Subregional Levels and Trends, *The Lancet* (2016), http://www.thelancet.com/journals/lancet/article/PIIS0140-6736(16)30380-4/abstract.
10. In 2016, the Policy was adjusted to allow 2 Children, but only when the

In 2007, Zhang Weiqing, minister in charge of the National Population and Family Planning Commission in China declared the success of the OCP in this way: "Because China has worked hard over the last thirty years, we have 400 million fewer people."[11] That is a round-about way of saying the OCP has resulted in the intentional killing of 400 million innocent unborn babies.

If you can only have one child, there are cultural and economic reasons why that child must be a boy. The biologically natural sex ratio is 105, which means that 105 boys are born for every 100 girls. That figure is also represented as 105:100.

In 1979, the sex ratio in China was 106:100.

After thirty-one years of the OCP, China's sex ratio in 2010 was 118:100.[12]

Whatever short-term benefits there were in terms of economic growth, the long-term implications are devastating for society and present enormous challenges and opportunities for the gospel.

The Chinese government estimates that by 2020, there will be at least 30 million men of marriageable age that may be unable to find a spouse.[13]

But research in the British Medical Journal reported in 2009, that China already had 32 million more men under 20 than women.[14]

According to research done by All Girls Allowed, "China alone stands to have as many unmarried young men—known as "bare branches"—as the entire population of young men in America. At present, there are 40 million American men under 20. In 2020, the Chinese Academy of Social Sciences estimates that there will be 40 million more Chinese men than women in that same age group."[15]

> Underneath the anticipated social upheaval that today's baby boys face as they become young men in search of wives lies the unspeakable evil of baby girls being targeted for death. The most dangerous place in the word today for girls in China is the womb. The *Economist* magazine calls it "*Gendercide: The war on*

---

government approves of it. For example, a single woman, carrying her first or second child will not be allowed to give birth legally. She will not be able to receive a birth permit or a "hukou," a registration form that permits the child to obtain medical, educational and other benefits.

11. Bristow, "Has China's One-Child Policy Worked?"
12. Kang and Wang. "Sex Ratio at Birth."
13. U.S. Congressional-Executive Commission on China.
14. BMJ Publishing Group, "China's Excess Males."
15. All Girls Allowed, "Gendercide China Statistics."

baby girls, and states, *"Killed, aborted or neglected, at least 100 million girls have disappeared—and the number is rising."*[16] "

For many women, the prospect of forced abortion is simply too much. Congressman Christopher Smith, in Congressional hearings, stated, "According to the most recent State Department Human Rights Report, one consequence of [China's] 'birth limitation policies' is that 56 percent of the world's female suicides occur in China, which is five times the world average, and approximately 500 suicides by women per day."[17]

And of course, the rarer something is, the more valuable it becomes. The trafficking of infant girls is another evil rippling out from the crime of child-killing.

THE PENETRATING AND DISRUPTIVE POWER OF THE CHRISTIAN VIEW OF HUMAN VALUE

We assert that all human life is valuable and belongs to God because all people are made in the image of God (Genesis 1:27). Since every human being is created in the image of God, every human being has *intrinsic* value. Since God created both male and female in his image, of every race, human beings have *equal* value. Since it is only human beings that are made in God's image, human life has *exceptional* value. As Dr. Marc Newman once said, "It makes a difference whether you kill the pig to feed the child or kill the child to feed the pig." Finally, we speak of *eternal* value; for every human being is created, in terms of God's moral will, to be like him in holiness and be with him in eternity.

The moral offense of abortion begins here. If the unborn is a member of the human family, then killing him or her to benefit others is a serious moral wrong. It treats the distinct human being, with his or her own inherent moral worth, as nothing more than a disposable instrument. Conversely, if the unborn are not human, killing them for any reason requires no more justification than having a tooth pulled.

It is true that the word "abortion" is not mentioned in the Bible. But neither is the word "lynching" or "genocide." The Bible condemns them all as the intentional killing of innocent human beings. In biblical language, abortion represents another expression of "the shedding of innocent blood" and marks a people with "blood-guilt" (Dt 21:1–9).

---

16. *The Economist*, "Gendercide."
17. Women's Rights without Frontiers, "Forced Abortion is not a Choice."

The moral crisis of abortion provides two major entry points for the gospel. The first is pregnancy crisis intervention, where you are hearing women and couples explain why being pregnant in their present circumstances feels overwhelming to them.

A pregnancy-related crisis is always a crisis of faith. This view is not limited to Christian worldview advocates. The standard textbook, *Crisis Intervention Strategies*, now in its 8th edition, reports,

> *"Faith plays a huge role in the outcome of a crisis as people attempt to make sense of events that seemingly make no sense at all. Faith plays a large part in how people try to come to terms with a randomly cruel universe that crashes down on the notion of a supreme being that runs a just and moral world.*
>
> *"Many human services workers regard it as an exposed electrical wire, not to be touched on pain of death for fear they will be seen as either proselytizing for their religion or insensitive to other spiritual beliefs[;] however, to deny or act as if religion, faith, or spirituality are not part of any crisis, is to neglect a large part of a crisis response for most people. . .it is interesting that little space is given to the effects that religion has in the counseling business. Yet for most people trauma is the ultimate challenge to meaning making, and for most people, that meaning making is attached to some kind of faith."*[18]

It is not surprising then that people of faith are very good at addressing people without hope. Helping them find a life-affirming solution often proves to be a life-changing experience. To choose life is an expression of faith. It may start out vaguely, but in helping people through a crisis pregnancy, you are asking them to trust in God. You are showing them how to pray for his provision of daily bread. They see amazing love in your concern and have many opportunities to hear how Christ has changed your life and can change their own.

AFTER-ABORTION TRAUMA AND THE GOSPEL

The second entry point for the gospel is afforded in helping people *after* abortion find a gospel solution to the guilt and grief that plagues them. For many, abortion is the one thing that most stains their conscience and alienates them from God.

---

18. Gilliland and James, *Crisis Intervention Strategies*, 42.

Perhaps the best way to understand the gospel opportunities surrounding abortion is to begin with the actual voices of those who have experienced a pregnancy-related crisis and turned to abortion as the solution.

Michaelene writes,

> When I became pregnant at 18, my first thought was to have an abortion. The abortion would allow me to continue teaching ballroom dance and training for competition. The idea of adoption did cross my mind. I knew I wasn't ready to parent, but I thought perhaps I could delay my career for the nine months or so that it would take me to carry my baby to term. My 28-year-old live-in boyfriend was furious when he discovered I was pregnant. He immediately demanded that I have an abortion. . .
>
> I didn't have any other friends or contacts in the area, so I decided to seek advice from the [dance] studio manager. After I told her about my situation, she recommended abortion and offered to arrange one for me. I left the office with the date and the time of the appointment and an arranged ride from my supervisor. . .
>
> Although I didn't feel this way before the procedure, it was now clear to me that the abortion ended the life of my child. I felt guilty and desired punishment. I deserved to suffer. Afterward, the mere presence of my boyfriend caused deep hurt and pain. I found it difficult to work. . .I soon found myself in a cycle of self-destructive behavior that included an eating disorder.[19]

Michaelene testifies to the trauma that many (though not all) women suffer from after-abortion Post Traumatic Stress Disorder (PTSD). As one women told me in an unforgettable way, "We are connected to our babies by an umbilical cord that is not just physical, but emotional, psychological and spiritual. When we kill our babies, we kill ourselves."

But abortion affects men and marriages too. Brad writes,

> My wife and I found out she was pregnant shortly after we were married. We were both very excited! We believed the baby was going to be a little boy. We were going to name him Trevor.
>
> Tracey started suffering from severe morning sickness. She decided she couldn't go through with the pregnancy. She said, "I'm going to get an abortion. I'm having one no matter what you say or do."[20]
>
> I didn't argue with her. I tried to support her decision. I secretly hoped that my compassion and prayer would change her

---

19. Fredenburg, *Changed*, 6–8.
20. Ibid., 20–21.

> *mind. However, when I think about it now, I think I could have done more to help her think through her decision.*
>
> *When Tracey came out after the abortion, she looked worse than before she went in. It looked as though the life had been sucked out of her. I did what I could to make her comfortable.*
>
> *Tracey and I divorced, and we soon lost contact with each other. When I talked to her many years later, she brought up the abortion and started crying. She said she'd gone through therapy.*

Finally, let us hear from a woman recalling her teen pregnancy.

> *My family would not support my decision to keep the baby. My boyfriend said he would give me no emotional or financial help whatsoever. All the people that mattered told me to abort. When I said I didn't want to, they started listing reasons why I should. That it would have detrimental effects on my career, and my health, and that I would have no social life and no future with men. . . .I'm so angry at myself for giving in to the pressure of others.*[21]

These voices give credence to the research regarding abortion's impact on mental health. According to the research, abortion renders people *everywhere* grief stricken, regretful, depressed, and self-loathing. Examining abortion-related PTSD, the deVeber Institute for Bioethics and Social Research sifted through 650 extensively researched and published papers in medical and psychological journals. The researchers provide their conclusions in the book, *Complications: Abortion's Impact on Women*. Regarding the psychological, emotional and spiritual impact of abortion, they conclude that "the increase in the rate of depression, anxiety, substance abuse and suicide among women who have had an abortion is drastic and incontrovertible."[22]

How drastic? They point to the meta-analysis research of Priscilla Coleman as especially weighty.[23] Coleman's methods, criteria, and controls were sufficient to have her research published in the peer-reviewed *British Journal of Psychiatry* in 2011. "Her review of these studies strongly supported an association between abortion and mental health problems. She discovered an overall 81 percent greater risk of mental health problems for women who had an abortion compared to those who did not."[24]

In her article, Coleman summarized the type of risks and the increased risk percentage as follows:

21. Reardon, *Aborted Women*, 31.
22. Lanfranchi, Gentles, and Ring-Cassidy, *Complication*, 255.
23. Coleman, "Abortion and Mental Health," 180–86.
24. Lanfranchi, Gentles, and Ring-Cassidy, *Complications*, 273.

- Anxiety disorders—34 percent
- Depression—37 percent
- Alcohol use/abuse—110 percent
- Marijuana use/abuse—220 percent
- Suicide behaviors—155 percent[25]

Are these not *all* expressions of the human condition that the gospel comes to address and the gospel alone can heal?

IMPLICATIONS FOR CHINA AND THE GOSPEL

Almost every expert on contemporary China fails to calibrate for the impact of abortion on a society. A few have mentioned the demographic challenges facing China as fertility rates continue to fall far below replacement level fertility. But I assert that any accurate understanding of China today must consider the impact of abortion, infanticide and gendercide, as well as the utilitarian and "capacity" view of human value from which it comes.[26]

Imagine heading over to Germany in 1946 and not asking how war has impacted the people. More specifically, what would it mean to serve the cause of the gospel in the town of Dachau? Would you not need to consider how the reality of bloodguilt has affected the population you are serving? If you avoided, rather than addressed how the death of Christ on the cross can atone (cover over) even the murder of innocents, would anything else you say really matter?

---

25. Ibid., 274.

26. The *capacity* view, properly known as the *property* view of human life limits human value, and thus human rights, to those who demonstrate certain capacities. For example, Mary Ann Warren, writes in "On the Moral and Legal Status of Abortion" *"I suggest that the traits which are most central to the concept of personhood, or humanity in the moral sense, are, very roughly; the following:*

1. consciousness (of objects and events external and/or internal to the being), and in particular the capacity to feel pain;

2. reasoning (the developed capacity to solve new and relatively complex problems);

3. self-motivated activity; 4. the capacity to communicate 5. the presence of self-awareness. . .

All we need to claim, to demonstrate that a fetus is not a person, is that any being which satisfies none of the above is certainly not a person. A man or woman whose consciousness has been permanently obliterated but who remains alive is a human being which is no longer a person; defective human beings, with no appreciable mental capacity, are not and presumably never will be people; and a fetus is a human being which is not yet a person, and which therefore cannot coherently be said to have full moral rights." The Problem of Abortion, ed. Joel Feinberg (Belmont, CA: Wadsworth, 1984).

Failure to wrestle with these questions, or worse, avoiding the discomfort of talking about the shedding of innocent blood, would mean fundamentally failing to find the entry point God has created for the gospel to be utterly glorified in its expiating and propitiating power.

Similarly, I met a man once who told me, "God can never forgive me. I killed my wife." I realized then that some experiences mark people in specific ways.

In his case, general gospel assurances about God's love on the cross would not help him. He needs a response to his bloodguilt that gnaws at him with specificity—memories of exact times and places, certain sounds and smells that continually bear witness against him. To help this man I need to bring the cross to bear on this *one* evil act that has convinced him that God could not forgive him and remain a just God.

I need to explain the cross as the shedding of innocent blood that can purge away even the guilt of shedding innocent blood. I needed to press him further, and show him that if he were to trust in the substitutionary punishment of Christ *as his own*, as full penalty paid for the full punishment due, then the justice of God that now condemns him will henceforth defend him; for a just God can not punish the same sin twice.

We do not meet many people on the street marked by the bloodguilt of wife-killing. But every day we do interact with people marked by another specific kind of bloodguilt—abortion. At current rates in the US, 33 percent of all women will have one abortion by the age of 45.[27] That means one-third of all men are also directly touched by and coping with the blood-guilt of abortion. In China, the OCP has probably rendered well over half the adult population quietly but surely conscience stricken with no place to go for relief.

To be sure, in China today, we are talking to a people marked by abortion, infanticide and gendercide. One of the major entry points of the gospel then is to speak to the bloodguilt people already feel, or that exposure to the truth of abortion quickly arouses. The matter is not too sensitive to bring up. Rather it is the one place where people are most sensitive to their need for forgiveness.

Pregnancy crisis intervention in China

From Han Chinese students at Beijing University, who are locked in a materialistic world view, to Uighur Muslim women in Xining, who are controlled by strict religious rules, people find themselves in crisis pregnancy.

27. Guttmacher Institute, "Facts on Induced Abortion in the United States."

One of the most effective ways to engage people walled off by disinterest or religion is to find and serve people who are in crisis. It's worth repeating, the reason medical missions was always an effective entry point I because sick people are searching people. Likewise, today's Christian counseling centers attract people in personal or family crisis. These centers are seeing ample opportunity to bring Christ to the crisis.

The work of pregnancy crisis intervention is proving to be similarly effective as people come for help. The Lozier Institute reports,

In 2017, pregnancy centers provided nearly 2,000,000 people in the United States with free services, with estimated community cost savings of at least $161 million annually. Women, youth, and men received services including pregnancy tests, options consultation, sexual risk avoidance education, parenting and prenatal education, ultrasound and medical services, community referrals, and material support. These vital services were provided at no cost to clients.[28]

Within minutes, the person who comes to talk to you about her crisis pregnancy is telling you personal, even intimate, details of her life. You, in turn, are asking her invasive questions you would never ask under normal circumstances. For examples, you may need to ask about her recent sexual behavior, prior pregnancies and outcomes, the nature of her relationship with her partner, her deepest values, her religious beliefs, and why being pregnant at this time is so distressing. All of this is context for bringing Christ to the crisis of abortion.

I've worked with numerous PHOs in both the US and China. Among the counselors the saying goes, "Help a mother save her baby, and watch! By the grace of God, the baby will save the mother."

In China, a movement started in 2012 to teach questions to pastors on bioethics, abortion and pregnancy intervention. The four questions were:

1. What does God say about human life, including life in the womb?
2. What does God say about the shedding of innocent blood, including abortion?
3. How do we bring the grace of the gospel to the guilt of abortion, so that people are forgiven and set free?
4. What does God call us to do to stop the shedding of innocent blood and how have others done so?

In 2014 and 2015, three of the largest networks of unregistered churches organized a campaign to teach 3 million people these 4 questions. They

---

28. Charlotte Lozier Institute, "A Half Century of Hope," 11.

called it the Children's Day Campaign as it was designed to be completed on June 1st, Children's Day in China.

The "Uncles," as the network leaders are called, wanted to see their people embrace the biblical view of human value, reject abortion as the shedding of innocent blood, and summon their people to help their pregnant neighbors.

Hundreds of "rescue" stories followed. Not surprising, many of them include how the mothers or the parents or the husband came to Christ through the intervention.

One of the earliest I witnessed was in Beijing. Two Christian women brought their pregnant neighbor to a 4 Questions training. She was pregnant with her second child in violation of the policy at that time. The two Christian women said to the pastors, "Her husband is forcing her, threatening to leave, if she does not follow the policy and abort. But we are going to be like the midwives of Egypt!"

This was a reference to the applied bioethics lived out by Israel during their oppressive bondage in Egypt, including a law of forced-child-killing. Exodus 1:22 says, "So Pharaoh commanded all his people, saying, 'Every son who is born you shall cast into the river.'"

The women were recalling the faithful witness of Exodus 1:17, "The midwives feared God and did not do as the king of Egypt commanded them, but let the male children live." The "midwives of Egypt!" became their watchword for pregnancy crisis intervention.

A year later, these sisters gave an update: "The husband abandoned his wife. He was afraid to violate the policy. But we stuck with her! We were there when the baby was born. Our whole neighborhood watched us, and so did her husband. He became a Christian."

I have such anecdotal accounts from Hefei, Shanghai, Lanzhou, Yantai, Harbin, Xining, and the other 30–40 cities where I have seen an applied bioethical approach used to address pregnancy crisis and abortion grief. Clearly, pregnancy help ministry is becoming a global missions movement. As you plan your approach, prayerfully consider how prolife work, done with courage and compassion, is a major entry point for engaging the culture.

Chapter 5

Social Service Ministry in China

Swells in the Middle Kingdom

While social service has long been part of missionary work in Mainland China, today a host of different factors are driving Chinese Christians to explore for themselves the place of humanitarian concerns within gospel ministry. For a growing number of local Christians, loving one's neighbor through acts of service is rapidly becoming an indispensible aspect of Christian witness. This essay will first explore the role of social service in the history of mission in China before analyzing its place in the ministry of the contemporary Chinese church. Given current conditions in China, some details must be left out of the discussion of the contemporary situation.

In the winter of 2016 I participated in a conference in Hong Kong hosted by several different China ministry agencies designed to help Mainland Chinese church leaders get a better understanding of what was happening on a macro level within the Chinese church across the country. Presentations on topics such as Christian home schools, Chinese seminaries, Chinese cross-cultural mission, and the future role of expatriates in China ministry were given by various thought-leaders—most of them Chinese Christians from the mainland. Over the course of the multi-day symposium, attendees were divided into various working groups designed to focus attention and ideally coalesce opinions on a select number of hot issues.

One of the working groups was tasked with summarizing the state of social concern (*shehui guanhuai* 社会关怀) ministries within the Mainland Chinese Christian community. A large number of mainland attendees had elected to join this group, and when it came time to present their work at the end of the conference, their representative stood up and delivered an impassioned defense of the need for the church in China to engage more deeply in activities that demonstrated social concern for their local communities. Many voices rose in assent, and heads nodded around the room in eager agreement. During the question and answer time, however, it quickly emerged that the members of this group—while all agreeing that churches across the country needed to demonstrate social concern—were nevertheless deeply divided on the relative importance of these kinds of activities. For a small number of attendees social concern was a vital aspect of spreading the gospel (*chuan fuyin* 传福音) while for many of those present it was a sideline task—strategic, perhaps, but quite different from actual gospel ministry. The group's presentation to the conference thus ended in confusion, with different attendees speaking at and across one another in debate over the relationship between social service (*shehui fuwu* 社会服务) and evangelism (*chuan fuyin* 传福音).

SOCIAL SERVICE AND EVANGELISM

Social services are generally understood to include any activities designed to promote social well being or, more narrowly, any programs that offer organized philanthropic assistance. From a ministry perspective, these are the sorts of activities that intentionally (though not exclusively) address various this-worldly needs. Educational initiatives, disaster relief, economic assistance, medical aid, legal or political advocacy, psychological counseling, and a host of other activities have been undertaken by Christians throughout history and around the world—all with the intent of advancing the cause of the gospel. Theologically, these kinds of ministries are grounded in a belief that all aspects of life are part a Christian's witness, in as much as the living gospel, as communicated through Word, deed, and sign, must necessarily be expressed through or embodied in actual lives. In many cases, the conviction that the Kingdom of God has implications for human life on this earth provides a key justification for Christians engaging in the provision of social services. More recently, the acknowledgment that evangelism and conversion are only steps—albeit critical steps—along the lifelong path of discipleship, has become an integral part of this emerging understanding of what is now commonly referred to as holistic mission.[1]

---

1. For a helpful summary of holistic mission, see Mark Russell, "Christian Mission Is Holistic," *International Journal of Frontier Missions* 25, no. 2 (2008): 93–98. The ideas in this paragraph are taken from Bryant L. Myers's classic modern text on Christian social engagement, *Walking with the Poor: Principles and Practices of Transformational*

The question of how social service relates to evangelism has been raised periodically throughout Christian history, despite the persistent instances of integration. Building on the example of Jesus's own ministry, early Christians carried on his understanding of the Kingdom of God by caring for the poor, the widows, and the orphans—not only in their own fellowships but in society as well.[2] The remarkable practical care provided by Christians during some of the early epidemics that ravaged the Mediterranean was a key factor—alongside Christian recognition of women as important social actors imbued with the image of God—in the rapid growth and spread of Christianity in the first few centuries of the church.[3] When the global Protestant mission movement took its earliest steps twelve hundred years later, pietistic Moravian Christians were at the forefront, leading the way from Bohemia to North and South America, Latin America, Africa, and eventually Asia. Their conviction that "service of souls" and "service of the body" were interdependent aspects of gospel ministry ensured that education and social concern were integral components of their early mission program.[4]

The Jesuit mission to China is today commonly remembered for its presence at the imperial court beginning in the final years of the Ming Dynasty and its successful outreach to the scholarly elite of the sixteenth- and seventeenth-centuries. Recent studies, however, have drawn attention to the comparatively greater amount of energy expended by most Jesuit missionaries in caring for common people amongst the many rural communities where their churches were established. The earliest baptized converts of the Jesuit mission were common "women, children, the sick and the old," many of whom had experienced miracles while having their physical needs addressed by the foreign priests.[5]

From its earliest beginnings with the 1807 arrival of Robert Morrison in Guangzhou, Protestant missions in China have been involved in a host of activities besides the oral proclamation of the gospel. From Robert Morrison's dictionary work to S. Wells Williams's printing press; from Peter Parker's ophthalmic hospital to the opium refuge work of the Oberlin Band in rural Shanxi; missionaries on the field time and again were compelled by their circumstances and the needs of the people around them to do more

---

Development (Maryknoll, NY: Orbis Books, 1999), especially chapter 8.

2. Even amongst proponents of social service ministry, Gal 6:10 is often used to support prioritizing service within the church over service in the larger community.

3. Stark, *The Rise of Christianity*.

4. Bosch, *Transforming Mission*, 254–55.

5. Laven, *Mission to China*, 55, 195–97, 212–21.

than merely speak the gospel in words.⁶ The classic dichotomy between Hudson Taylor's gospel work amongst common people and Timothy Richard's educational work amongst China's elite is itself a gross caricature of nineteenth-century evangelical mission in China: Taylor employed medical and educational work in his mission even as Richard presented the gospel message through spoken and written words to large swaths of famine-oppressed Chinese farmers.⁷ The nineteenth-century anti-opium crusading of many of the China missionaries was a natural outgrowth of their evangelistic encounters with opium users on the China field, and many of their supporters embraced the cause back in Britain, successfully lobbying Parliament to outlaw the trade.⁸ This kind of activism, in the form of political reform, orphanages, Sunday School educational programs, health crusades, temperance movements—all the services the Salvation Army undertook and more—has long been an identifying feature of evangelical Christianity.⁹ The institution building that became such a prominent feature of late nineteenth- and early twentieth-century Christian missions in China enshrined this activism in the many hospitals, orphanages, and schools established to extend those social service ministries to more and more people.¹⁰

The North American Fundamentalist-Modernist debates of the early twentieth century left their mark on the China mission world as well, as a growing number of western missionaries began to eschew the more supernatural aspects of the Kingdom of God for a very this-worldly sense of mission.¹¹ Taking over the language of "Social Gospel" that had previously captured the quite opposite conviction of Victorian evangelicals that their faith should find expression in active concern for the poor conditions of others in society, these missionaries to China reduced the missionary task to humanitarian projects alone.¹² At the same time, eminent Chinese Chris-

6. Nat Brandt, *Massacre in Shansi* (New York: toExcel, 1999); Christopher Daily, *Robert Morrison and the Protestant Plan for China* (Hong Kong: Hong Kong University Press, 2013); Andrew T. Kaiser, "S. Wells Williams: Early Protestant Missions in China " (MA Thesis, Gordon-Conwell Theological Seminary, 1995).

7. Kaiser, *Encountering China*.

8. Weber, "Abolish This Great Evil," 216–30.

9. Activism is one of the four defining features of David Bebbington's well-known evangelical quadrilateral, alongside biblicism, conversionism, and crucicentrism. David W. Bebbington, *Evangelicalism in Modern Britain: A History from the 1730s to the 1980s* (London: Unwin Hyman, 1989; reprint, New York: Routledge, 2002), 2–3.

10. Hyatt, "Protestant Missions in China," 93–126.

11. Xi, *The Conversion of Missionaries*.

12. On Victorian British understandings of the Social Gospel, see Brian Stanley, "Evangelical Social and Political Ethics: An Historical Perspective," *Evangelical Quarterly* 62, no. 1 (1990): 19–36.

tians such as T. C. Chao (Zhao Zichen) and Y. T. Wu (Wu Yaozong) were likewise arguing that the Chinese church must concern itself with China's social development.[13] And yet for those missionaries in China—whether local or expatriate—who insisted on the abiding spiritual significance of faith in Jesus, integration of evangelism and social service continued to be a practical, and often theological, necessity for their ministry. Anna Ziese, an Assemblies of God missionary who served for forty-nine years in twentieth-century China, is considered a legend for her faithful presence in China up until her death in 1969. Her most noted ministry involved evangelism *and* visitation in the Taiyuan, Shanxi prison.[14]

Drawing on ideas developed within Latin American theology, the 1974 First International Congress on World Evangelization held in Lausanne, Switzerland gave expression to a newly revived evangelicalism that rejected the either-or dichotomy of the earlier Fundamentalist-Modernist debates to espouse a robust Kingdom theology that integrated oral proclamation and social service within the evangelistic task.[15] As more and more mission agencies around the world joined the Lausanne community, its evolving advocacy for "the whole church taking the whole gospel to the whole world" became representative of large portions of the evangelical mission world.[16] The missions community continues to debate constructively the relative priority and importance of evangelism versus humanitarian aid, but for younger generations of (short- and long-term) missionaries ideals similar to the original Moravian impulse to serve souls *and* bodies are increasingly important motivations for service.[17] Whether or not these new generations of missionaries will be able to hold these two impulses in healthy tension, or fall into either of the dualistic extremes of the early twentieth century, remains to be seen.

---

13. Chow, *Chinese Public Theology*, 40–41.

14. David Bundy, "Anna Ziese: For God and China," *Assemblies of God Heritage* 20, no. 3 (2000): 13–21. See also Andrew T. Kaiser, "Anna Ziese" in *Biographical Dictionary of Chinese Christianity*, http://bdcconline.net/en/stories/anna-ziese.

15. On integrative mission in Latin American evangelicalism, see David C. Kirkpatrick, "C. René Padilla and the Origins of Integral Mission in Post-War Latin America," *The Journal of Ecclesiastical History* 67, no. 2 (2016).

16. From section six of "The Lausanne Covenant" in James Dixon Douglas, *Let the Earth Hear His Voice: International Congress on World Evangelization, Lausanne, Switzerland, Official Reference Volume, Papers and Responses* (Minneapolis: World Wide Publications, 1975), 3–9.

17. On the central role of the service project in narratives of North American short-term missions trips, see Brian M. Howell, *Short-Term Mission: An Ethnography of Christian Travel Narrative and Experience* (Downers Grove, IL: IVP Academic, 2012), 184–88.

When expatriate missionaries began returning to China in numbers in the early1980s, restrictions on foreign religious activity forced many Christian organizations and individuals to establish businesses and social service organizations as some of the few means available to secure extended residence in China. China's stage of development made many of the offered services, such as English training, agricultural and medical services, disaster and poverty relief projects, and community development, quite attractive to Chinese officials eager for their nation to "catch up" with the rest of the world.[18] For those expatriate Christians who served in China during the first decade of opening and reform, memories of successful official banquets facilitated by all parties' shared commitment to "Serve the People (*wei renmin fuwu* 为人民服务)" are still strong, though perhaps not as strong as their recollections of the many Chinese people who came to Jesus through the services that were provided. As the ministry roles of expatriates shifted over the next forty years from *leading* their own ministry initiatives to *partnering* with local Christians and, in recent years, *serving* under the direction of Chinese Christian leaders, these expatriates have had a profound influence on the way many younger Chinese Christians view social service ministry. Chinese believers are increasingly aware of the vast array of social services provided by local and foreign Christians in China during the nineteenth and early twentieth centuries; but the example of the foreign Christians they have personally known is encouraging many of today's Chinese Christians to care for their communities in the name of Jesus.

SOCIAL SERVICE AND TODAY'S CHINESE CHURCH

On a recent trip to Chengdu I was able to visit five different social service ministries. In each case, these were projects run by local believers. They each had their own form of local legal registration, and they were primarily relying on monies collected in China to fund their project expenses. Some were more like companies, others more like charities; some were urban in their focus, others more rural; most were in some sort of partnership with a government entity. But in each case I was left with the overwhelming impression that these Chinese projects were doing the very same kinds of things that foreign social service workers had been doing across China in the late 1990s and early 2000s. Certainly, for reasons outlined below, Chengdu is

---

18. For a recent analysis of some of the factors that shape official attitudes towards faith-based charity work in China, see Susan K. McCarthy, "In between the Divine and the Leviathan: Faith-Based Charity, Religious Overspill and the Governance of Religion in China," *The China Review* 17, no. 2 (2017): 65–93.

at the forefront of Christian social service ministry; but even so this marks an inflection point for the church in China. In officially registered churches and house church networks across the nation, believers are expressing interest in incorporating social service into their ministry activities.

Many older Chinese Christians today can recall back in the 1990s when it was not unusual to see a small clinic attached to a registered church, often staffed by retired medical workers from the congregation. A few unofficial orphanages also existed, with members from a local house church or registered church caring for ten or so abandoned children outside of the official social welfare system. As Christians became more confident regarding their place in society, and as more and more Christians gained financial security, the scope for Christian social service began to expand. At first, most of these new initiatives were driven and managed by individuals within local congregations. By the early 2000s, various educational, medical, and economic relief projects were initiated—many operating informally, some involving legally registered entities. HIV-work, assistance for people with disabilities, financial aid for church construction in remote or impoverished locations, and various educational projects were soon being operated by Christians in many different locations across the country.

The series of earthquakes that struck western China from 2008 to 2014 ushered in a new era in Chinese Christian social service. Unable to ignore the desperate needs right on their doorsteps, churches throughout Sichuan were able to overcome their natural inclination to look inwards, and finally establish new habits of community engagement, even as these same disaster conditions rendered the state relatively open to grassroots participation in social action.[19] For the first time in modern memory, massive numbers of Chinese from all across the country volunteered to assist with the disaster relief efforts, flooding Wenchuan County and the surrounding area with eager if often naïve would-be "helpers."[20] While non-Christian young people were also moved to participate, Christians made up the majority of these volunteers, many choosing to remain and continue assisting long after others had left.[21] In one Sichuan hospital Christian volunteers organized

19. For more on the "consensus crisis" that allowed for the flourishing of Christian social services in the wake of the 2008 Sichuan earthquake, see Easten Law, "Faith-Based Engagement in China's Harmonious Society: A Study of an Indigenous, Faith-Based Ngo's Organizational Culture and Response to the 2008 Sichuan Earthquake," in *Shaping Christianity in Greater China: Indigenous Christians in Focus*, ed. Paul Woods (Oxford: Regnum Books International, 2017), 274–80.

20. One China Development Brief study suggests 263 foreign and domestic NGOs participated in the 2008 disaster relief efforts in Sichuan. Quoted in Law, "Faith-Based Engagement in China's Harmonious Society," 275.

21. Fulton, *China's Urban Christians*, 67–69.

themselves into a band of assistants with matching "Jesus Loves You" pins on their shirts, providing water, clothing, and basic assistance to the flood of patients seeking emergency medical services. Within a few days hospital staff had come to rely on these trustworthy, caring individuals, telling inquirers with simpler questions or problems to go ask a "little Jesus (*xiao Yesu* 小耶稣)" for help.[22]

The visible participation of Christians in the earthquake relief effort had a generally positive effect on public opinion and on the Christian population, which experienced a marked growth in conversions in the years following the disaster. However, the outpouring of Christian volunteers and charitable relief during the Sichuan earthquake also revealed the church's inexperience with social service ministry. Determined not to squander this opportunity to share their faith with their fellow citizens, some groups of Christian volunteers took advantage of peoples' traumatized state to coerce them to convert, employing techniques such as requiring people to recite a prayer accepting Jesus before they were given food or other kinds of aid. These instances of compassionless social service left some of the disaster-struck areas with a very unfavorable impression of Christianity.[23]

While saddening, this phenomenon is not entirely surprising. When the Chinese church recommenced public worship in the early 1980s, many aspects of Christian faith and practice still showed the hallmarks of an inherited fundamentalist theology. For many older Chinese Christians, their life-long experience of Christian discipleship had been profoundly shaped by the influence of conservative foreign missionaries and Chinese evangelists from the 1930s and 1940s whose own theology was colored by the Fundamentalist-Modernist controversy. This is at least part of the reason behind the more otherworldly understandings of Christian witness that are popularly held by older Chinese believers. For this generation of Christians, social service is distinct from the oral proclamation of the gospel; it smacks of the "Social Gospel" and represents a distraction of energies and resources from the primary task of evangelism.[24] The parallels with North American debates from the previous century are striking.

The testimonies of younger Christians, however, often feature contemporary expatriate Christians—many of whom are or were engaged at least publicly in the delivery of various public or professional services.[25] For

22. This phenomenon was reported by the author's coworkers upon their return from providing medical assistance on site in the aftermath of the disaster.

23. Ma and Li, *Surviving the State*, 107.

24. For a typical example, see one pastor's critique of charitable work in Li and Jin, *Surviving the State, Remaking the Church*: 112.

25. See, for example, the role of foreign English teachers in the conversion of a

these newer believers who came to faith during the period of opening and reform, social service is seen as a more natural part of Christian identity in as much as so many expatriate examples of Christian living involved the provision of services such as English teaching, economic development, medical care, or disaster relief to people inside and outside the church. This generally positive impression, however, is in some cases muddled by expatriate Christians who—particularly during the earlier phases of post-opening and reform China ministry—justified shirking or downplaying their professional responsibilities in light of the urgency or importance of their "spiritual" ministry. Viewing their public identity as teachers, doctors, or aid workers as a "cover" or "platform," these expatriates often unintentionally gave the impression that their service to the community was of little gospel significance.[26] This kind of contradiction between what expatriate Christians said and what they actually did provides support in China for the lingering fundamentalist instinct to erect a theological dichotomy between social service and evangelism.

The massive outpouring of grass roots assistance from across the country during the 2008 Sichuan earthquake ultimately posed a challenge to the authority and legitimacy of local officials, and by 2011 the government had clamped down on the activities of foreign and grassroots organizations in the province.[27] Chinese social service providers responded by using existing laws to register their local projects—some charitable, some for profit, many of them Christian—as legal entities. This provided Sichuan, in particular, with a mature, effective, and local social service industry prior to January 1, 2017, when the new law for the administration of foreign NGOs came into force and effectively closed the door to social service ministry in China through foreign NGOs.[28] While initially regarded as an attempt to halt the development of social services in China, these regulatory measures are now viewed by many as an attempt to reshape emerging civil society in the image of the Party.[29] Under the new regulations, expatriate social service

---

Chinese doctor as recorded in chapter 8 of Liao Yiwu, *God Is Red: The Secret Story of How Christianity Survived and Flourished in Communist China* (New York: HarperCollins, 2011).

26. For a recent instance of a missionary grappling with this issue, see Elliot Clark, "The Non-Negotiable of Missionary Integrity," *The Gospel Coalition*, April 20, 2018, https://www.thegospelcoalition.org/article/non-negotiable-missionary-integrity/.

27. Details in this paragraph are from personal interviews with a registered Chinese Christian social organization (*shehui zuzhi* 社会组织) operating in Sichuan.

28. *The China NGO Project.* "Law of the People's Republic of China on Administration."

29. Shieh, "Remaking China's Civil Society."

organizations wishing to continue operating legally in China must complete a complicated registration process that requires the approval of one of a discrete number of officially sanctioned Professional Supervisory Units (*yewu zhuguan danwei* 业务主管单位); once registered, each individual event carried out by the foreign organization must also be separately approved by local Public Security officials. As of May 1, 2018, a little over 300 foreign NGOs (out of a 2016 total of between 1,000 and 7,000) have managed to successfully register representative offices in China.[30] This has left an unknown number of agencies to either leave China or continue struggling to secure the relevant permissions, all of which has contributed to a shift in the kinds of issues that foreign NGOs in China are addressing.[31] Local social service organizations are stepping in to fill the void.

Since the 2008 Olympics in Beijing, the number of expatriate Christian China workers has been decreasing. Attempts to "manage" society in the run-up to the games resulted in the removal of many foreign Christian individuals and organizations. Instability out west and the lack of consequences to the state for these expulsions spurred on further regulatory and ideological developments that continue to constrain the population of foreign Christians legally residing in China—as seen in the forced removal of expatriates from several international sending agencies in the fall of 2018.[32] In light of this demographic shift, Chinese believers are becoming the primary workers and initiators in the Christian social service sector. The expatriate-run relief and development ministries of the 1990s and early 2000s are now bearing fruit, with Chinese believers trained in those projects now leading local initiatives. As younger Chinese Christians take on greater responsibility in local churches, their previous exposure to the social service ministries of expatriate workers gives them a level of comfort with these new forms of ministry, making social service projects real options for more and more local congregations—particularly house church fellowships. In addition to the individuals within congregations who rely on the financial gifts and volunteers of their fellowships to run their personal ministries, individual churches are now undertaking their own forms of social service

---

30. *The China NGO Project.* "Will 2018 Be the Year of a Silent Foreign NGO Exodus?"

31. In practice, management of the registration process allows the state to encourage some forms of social service and to effectively stifle the provision of services that are antithetical to the Party's priorities. Jessica Batke and Chen Qi Hang, "Has the Foreign NGO Law Changed the Work of Foreign NGOs in China?" *The China NGO Project* (January 10, 2018), http://www.chinafile.com/ngo/analysis/has-foreign-ngo-law-changed-work-of-foreign-ngos-china.

32. Due to ongoing security concerns, data for this multi-province action is not yet available.

work, with "social concern (*shehui guanhuai* 社会关怀)" or "public benefit (*gongyi* 公益)" committees becoming increasingly common within registered and unregistered churches alike.

In addition to the various socially engaged ministries that have emerged since the beginning of the period of opening and reform, Chinese churches today are developing new ways to reach out to the disadvantaged in their communities. Ministries related to family counseling are extremely popular in Christian circles today, with marriage enrichment seminars and weekend "getaway" retreats, lay trainings in psychological counseling and family dynamics, private for-profit counseling centers, and "life education" trainings for youths spreading rapidly across the country. Some churches are electing to "adopt" private unregistered Christian orphanages, offering legal and regulatory assistance from members of their congregation as well as the financial support and volunteer staffing that the projects need in order to function. Projects designed to care for children (*liushou ertong* 留守儿童) left behind by migrant worker parents have become common features of rural and urban churches alike, especially within the last two years. Christian schools are proliferating rapidly, although they are mostly small in scale (around a dozen children), expensive (due to translated curriculum and low student-teacher ratios), and primarily aimed at serving the church.[33] Elder care is expanding as well: I recently visited a large registered church (over a thousand members) in a rural county seat that now operates two nursing homes in their town. Registered as a private business owned by one of the church elders, the elder care facilities are located on church property alongside the church's own small clinic, providing a total of three hundred residential beds at a reasonable price. One significant and telling indication of the growing interest among Chinese Christians in social service ministry: China's largest registered Christian charity, the Amity Foundation, has recently begun participating in charitable projects outside of China's borders.[34]

Contemporary Challenges

While interest is growing in social service ministry, particularly among young urban believers, significant hurdles still remain. For churches that have for many decades been focused on the survival and maintenance of their congregation in an environment hostile to faith, turning outward can

---

33. Though there are reports from different locations noting increased official challenges to Christian education projects in the second half of 2018.

34. This is clearly also a reflection of the Chinese church's growing interest in cross-cultural missions. See Part IV in this book.

be very challenging. The long-nurtured in-group mentality of so many congregations can make it difficult for them to embrace the kinds of external engagement that social service ministry entails. For those churches who do not already have local members who are practitioners or at least informed advocates for this kind of ministry, all the will in the world is often not enough to develop these new forms of outreach. In a dozen provinces across the country, local Christian social service workers are forming networks—associations of like-minded servants gathered to share resources, consult together on legal issues, hold each other accountable, and provide mutual encouragement and assistance. These fellowships are already being utilized by local and foreign organizations for the delivery of technical and theological training related to social service ministry. Local Christian social service incubators can offer valuable guidance and training in how to enter into social service ministry, functioning as a bridge to help churches cross over into the larger world of social service work; currently there are three such training centers operating with a national reputation.[35]

Chinese Christians already engaged in providing ministry through social services are quick to admit that the church still has much to learn about development principles and social service best practices. One Chinese relief worker recalled that on his first foray into disaster assistance in the Sichuan earthquake of 2008, he personally was responsible for organizing 512 Christian volunteers from all across China who arrived in the disaster area with the same idea: "show me where I can evangelize (*chuan fuyin* 传福音)!" Such thinking persists in many Chinese churches, with pastors and congregants unclear of how social service relates to evangelism or the gospel. One Chinese Christian social organization (*shehui zuzhi* 社会组织) was asked in 2014 to provide three to six months of training to a group of Chinese cross-cultural missionaries who had had their visas confiscated and been sent back to China owing to their "fundamentalist" approach to evangelism. Similarly, Christians in China typically have had little or no exposure to the basic principles behind transformational development or public benefit (*gongyi* 公益) projects, while even those already employed in social service ministries have yet to master industry best practices. As one experienced Chinese relief worker described things, most Chinese humanitarian workers still run around telling everyone "baby formula is great."[36] These stories, of course, all highlight just how new this kind of ministry remains for most Chinese churches.

35. Each possessing different strengths and foci, the three centers are located in Chengdu, Guangzhou, and Shanghai.

36. The details in this paragraph are from interviews with Christian social service workers in Sichuan. Many Chinese people believe baby formula—particularly imported baby formula—is superior to breast milk.

Legal registration also remains a challenge, owing to the frequent changes in government policies and implementation. There are currently four registration options for Chinese believers seeking to establish a legal basis for carrying out social services. Social associations (*shetuan* 社团) work well for organizing large groups of volunteers, but their financial operations and capabilities, including fund-raising, are extremely limited. Foundations (*jijinhui* 基金会) are for the most part restricted to giving away money, with an extremely high initial capital holdings requirement. Social service organizations (*shehui fuwu jigou* 社会服务机构) have replaced the previous civil non-enterprise units *(minban fei qiye* 民办非企业) as the primary channel for civil (non-government) non-profit operations in China, and they are further divided into four categories of activities: scientific (*keji* 科技), community services (*shequ fuwu* 社区服务), public benefit charities (*gongyi cishan* 公义慈善), and industrial and commercial associations (*hangye shangye xiehui* 行业商业协会).[37] These first three forms of legal registration are collectively known as "social organizations" (*shehui zuzhi* 社会组织 or *minjian zuzhi* 民间组织). The fourth registration option, public institutions (*shiye danwei* 事业单位), is restricted to government initiatives—the so-called GONGOs (government-organized non-governmental organizations).[38] Unfortunately, the requirements and processes for registration can vary greatly from region to region, with many civil affairs and public security officers making determinations on political factors that are far from transparent—and sometimes simply refusing to register any organizations at all.[39] Christian ministries often struggle to find an acceptable local entity to supervise their work (a requirement for most types of registration), in many cases tempting them to adopt deceptive practices to hide their religious connections in order to secure registration. Not surprisingly, some projects choose to simply register as a small business. While business registration is easy and the reporting process is comparatively standardized, this prevents ministries from raising local donations and receiving grants from most local foundations. Until the state further normalizes the role and especially the management of social service organizations in Chinese society, the legal status of all these efforts will remain precarious, limiting their development.

37. These four officially recognized categories for social service organization registration are from a 2018 interview with a Chinese consultant specializing in social service registration issues.

38. On current nomenclature, see "China," *Council on Foundations* (October 2017), https://www.cof.org/content/china#Types.

39. There are multiple reports of local officials refusing to process new applications for domestic social service organizations since January of 2019.

Finally, funding remains one of the biggest hurdles to widespread Christian participation in social service ministry. China's recent unprecedented levels of urbanization and economic growth have created many wealthy individuals within the Christian community. Unfortunately, the newfound nature of much of this prosperity has left little time for the development of biblical notions of stewardship and generosity within the church.[40] While it is not unusual to see churches financially supporting their own small-scale social service efforts, larger or more professional projects (city-wide education services, disaster relief and prevention initiatives, rural poverty alleviation, etc.) only rarely receive substantial, regular funding from churches.[41] The more developed and professional social service ministries tend to secure most of their funding by selling their services to the government or seeking grants from Chinese foundations. Having the government as a client definitely affects project selection and implementation, as some needed services or especially effective ways of serving are incompatible with government priorities. Likewise, while is it easier and much quicker to acquire funding from local foundations, they tend to give short-term grants and only support a portion of total expenses. An attempt was made in early 2018 to establish a legally registered national-level foundation with the cooperation of eight or nine Christian social service groups, but they were unable to secure approval in the face of what appeared to be a national-level unofficial halt to all foundation approvals.[42] For social service ministries to develop the Chinese church needs to discover more and better ways of financial support. Churches themselves need to catch a vision and develop practices for using their resources to support ministries beyond their own congregation.[43] It is too early to say whether or not the state will increase its willingness to purchase social services from local non-government providers, though experiments in Chengdu are encouraging. And without a national foundation that at least tacitly recognizes Christian priorities in the delivery of social services, many kinds of ministry will struggle to tap into bigger funding pools. The result is that for the time being many Christian social service operations that are not the product of a particular local congregation still rely on some degree of funding from

40. Fulton, "Will China Become Generous?"

41. Based on interviews with several more mature Chinese social service ministries.

42. From personal interviews with some of the participants.

43. The challenges here are similar to those faced by Chinese missionaries seeking financial support. Si Shi and GJ, "Financial Considerations in Chinese Missionary Sending: Sources of Support and Difficulties in Raising Finances," *ChinaSource* (April 20, 2017), https://www.chinasource.org/resource-library/articles/financial-considerations-in-chinese-missionary-sending.

outside China's borders. However, murky channels for outside funding and salaries paid for by foreigners are not long-term solutions for a church under increasing political and regulatory pressure to Sinicize (*zhongguohua* 中国化) and be truly independent.

CONCLUSION: HOPE FOR THE COMING WINTER

It is currently common to hear the phrase "winter is coming" repeated by church leaders from across China.[44] These words are being used by local Christians to describe their shared sense that the Chinese church is entering a period of increasing state persecution. As the Chinese Communist Party reinserts itself back into more and more sectors of Chinese society, traditional avenues for social service ministry are constricting. In 2019 orphans have been removed from private care and returned to the state-run social welfare institutes. The aggressive emphasis on political indoctrination through the state schooling system that rolled out in late 2018 has dramatically reduced the number of educational alternatives still in operation.[45] Combined with increasingly enforced restrictions on attendance at church for citizens under eighteen years of age, current trends suggest that opportunities to minister to children, in particular, will be very difficult to sustain in the near future. More darkly, some believe that the shocking "security measures" being employed by the Chinese state in Xinjiang are the future for "social management (*shehui guanli* 社会管理)" throughout the rest of China.[46] Over the past two or three years, international news services have recorded many signs of the state's growing determination to constrain Christian expression throughout Chinese society; but this important and significant trend cannot be adequately understood apart from an acknowledgment of the changes happening within the church as well. While the current push within the Mainland Chinese church to serve society in the name

---

44. Kaiser, "Chinese Christians Preparing for 'New Normal.'"

45. June Cheng, "Hard tests for China's Christian schools," *World Magazine* (September 13, 2018), https://world.wng.org/2018/09/hard_tests_for_china_s_christian_schools?platform=hootsuite. For an overview of the theoretical and historical underpinnings of China's current patriotic education drive, see "Homo Xinensis: Drop Your Pants! The Party Wants to Patriotise You All Over Again (Part III)," *China Heritage* (August 31, 2018), http://chinaheritage.net/journal/homo-xinensis/.

46. On security measures in Xinjiang, see Steven Jiang, "Chinese Uyghurs Forced To Welcome Communist Party into Their Homes," *CNN Online* (May 14, 2018), https://edition.cnn.com/2018/05/14/asia/china-xinjiang-home-stays-intl/index.html; Adrian Zenz and James Liebold, "Xinjiang's Rapidly Evolving Security State," *China Brief* 17, no. 4 (2017).

of Jesus has deep historic roots, several aspects of the church's contemporary condition suggest that China is on the cusp of a new era of Christian witness through the indigenous provision of social services.

First of all, as mentioned above, the number of expatriate Christians serving long-term in China has dropped dramatically since the Beijing Olympics. A systematic tightening of the regulations related to foreign residence, employment, and business activity in China has resulted in the departure of many expatriates—especially those involved in the provision of social services. Many project closures were long overdue, as foreign money and personnel had perpetuated ministries that were out of touch with the current Chinese context. In other cases, treasured ministries have come to an end, though it is hoped that in time local believers will preserve what is valuable from the legacy of those foreign efforts. Regardless, the signs are clear: the future of social service ministry in China lies in the hands of Chinese believers. Raising up a new generation of Chinese Christians to engage their communities for Christ should be top priority for existing expatriate and local social service providers.

Second, recent changes to China's regulatory environment have made it increasingly difficult for foreign social service ministries to secure the registrations and permits they need to operate legally within China. Increased surveillance of business activities, heightened financial controls, and the new foreign NGO law discussed above have made it difficult for many social service projects to maintain legal standing in China. While some of this reflects an actual increase in Chinese adherence to the rule of law, a recent government propaganda campaign highlights the decidedly political and even hostile motivation behind many of these actions. The Ministry of State Security and several other government institutions related to science and defense used the occasion of the third annual National Security Day on April 15, 2018 to promulgate a series of cartoons warning citizens to be wary of foreign spies masquerading as NGO workers.[47] While such ham-fisted security pushes are not new, this reveals the true nature of the state's apparent determination to control or eliminate foreigners working in China's social service sector. In this environment, every foreign social service initiative must be actively pursuing full localization of their ministry, supporting local believers in their efforts to establish, manage, and legally register their own indigenous social service ministries.[48]

---

47. *The China NGO Project.* "Government Cartoon Portrays 'Foreign NGOs' as National Security Threat."

48. Swells in the Middle Kingdom, "The Challenges of Localization."

Third, the growing tide of missionary sending from the Mainland Chinese church is also contributing to increased interest in social service ministry. Most obviously, the current Chinese church mania for short-term mission trips has created a demand for the kinds of "service projects" that many Christian social service initiatives represent. At the same time, the small but growing number of Chinese long-term cross-cultural missionaries are also receiving positive exposure to social service ministry as they encounter bi-vocational international ministry teams in hard-to-reach countries where social services are often important vehicles for engaging the local community and securing legal residence. As the ties between these Chinese missionaries and their sending churches strengthen, their experiences will likely filter down into the congregations, shaping and in some cases expanding believers' expectations of gospel ministry to include the provision of social services. Ideally, this will spur Chinese churches to develop new habits and mechanisms for supporting Chinese social service ministries through prayer, finances, and participation.

Fourth, many Christian leaders are deeply concerned about the shrinking role of the church in Chinese society. Between government propaganda and information control, and the pervasive presence of social media, Chinese people—particularly the young—seem to have little room for faith in their lives. Many local pastors see social service ministry and the community engagement it represents as a key pathway for demonstrating Christianity's continuing relevance for today's China. A new generation of Chinese people need to see and experience—as well as hear—the gospel for themselves. To remain focused on the survival of those already within the church walls, insulating the community of faith from the changing society, is to court marginalization. For many Chinese pastors, robust ministry through the provision of locally valued social services is necessary if the church hopes to reach present and future generations and avert fading into obscurity.[49]

Fifth, as religious affairs once again fall under the remit of the United Front Work Department, some Christians are looking for ways to justify their existence to the Party. With so little room within the China Dream for religious expression, there seems little reason for the Party to allow Christianity a place in society. While acknowledging that there will always be dissonance between the church and any worldly power, many church leaders see social service ministry as an opportunity to demonstrate the value of Christianity to Chinese society in a language that the Party can

---

49. This and the following paragraph are based on conversations with Chinese pastors in registered and unregistered churches in many different locations in China between 2016 and 2018.

understand and accept.[50] Consciously avoiding the naïve accommodationism of the early TSPM, today's Christians are looking for ways to faithfully preserve their public identity in this new Chinese epoch (*xin shidai* 新时代). This is a strategic attempt to preserve a sphere of civic space for the public demonstration of Christian faith—for gospel witness—in the face of growing restrictions.

As has happened so often in history, divine irony is employing the very conditions of state repression that are constricting the church's religious activities to lead the Chinese church into a new phase of gospel witness. While reports in the foreign media mourn the restrictions the Chinese church is facing and may increasingly face in the coming years, Chinese believers themselves are much more sanguine. During a conference I attended in 2016 one prominent mainland Christian intellectual directly addressed the threat of a coming winter. With a telling combination of confidence and sorrow in his expression, he reminded the attendees that the Chinese church has been through periods of repression in the past—and emerged in the end stronger than before. The same God who was faithful then is still in control, and he will preserve his church through whatever periods of suffering, purification, or growth he chooses to bring.

What is clear is that all these different factors—demographics, regulatory changes, theological developments, strategic considerations, political shifts, and more—have placed the church in a position where local believers increasingly will be called to step out of their comfort zones, independent of foreign assistance, and be the hands of Jesus in their communities. In many ways, the time has already arrived: as one Chinese author acknowledges, "Christianity has probably become China's largest nongovernmental organization."[51] This is a *kairos* moment, an opportunity for the church to offer an alternative to contemporary society. Care for society (*shehui guanhuai* 社会关怀) done faithfully can bring healing *shalom* through the building of trust and the demonstration of *agape* love to a cynical China where integrity seems impossible and all relationships feel broken. Even as the political winds blow strong in the face of the church, the witness of Chinese Christians through the provision of various social services holds the potential for gospel transformation—for a renewed China Dream that embodies the core values of the Kingdom of God.

---

50. One scholar notes that officials who value faith-based charity work as a "tradable resource" are often unaware of the degree to which Christian social service projects are able to transmit gospel messages through their service. McCarthy, "In between the Divine and the Leviathan," 72–73.

51. Li Fan, as quoted in Evan Osnos, "Five Things You Need to Know."

Chapter 6

Reaching China through Caring for Marginalized People

J. Haddon Bennett

INTRODUCTION

In the Tibetan city of Batang in western Sichuan there are apple orchards. These trees are not native to the area, but they have been a part of the community for one hundred years. They were planted by Dr. Albert Shelton and other members of the Tibet Christian Mission. These men and women left everything familiar in life to travel months by horseback, cross rivers, and avoid dangerous bandits to provide medical services to Chinese and Tibetan peoples.

Shelton was the first doctor to bring western medicine to Tibet. In order to supply the 50-bed hospital in Batang, 100 people would have to walk for 500 miles, from Chengdu to Batang. Shelton and his team brought vaccines, irrigation systems, and fruit trees to the area for the first time. Along with their medical services they preached the message of the Creator God and the gospel of Jesus. Dr. Shelton died and was buried there, just like many others going to this area of China. Most of their stories have not been passed down, and they will receive little recognition for their faithfulness this side of eternity.[1]

1. An extensive account of the Tibet Christian Mission can be found in *A Flame of the Fire: The Batang Tibetan Mission of the Disciples of Christ Missions* by Marian

Through much of the twentieth century missionary efforts across China were twofold — preach and heal.[2] Hospitals and orphanages were founded. The hungry were fed. The sick, disabled, and marginalized were shown care and respect by Christian foreigners. When missionaries sent back reports of conversions among Chinese people, these people were dismissed as "rice" Christians—men and women frequenting the missions only for the benefits that were provided there. Many western intellectuals believed that the Chinese were immune to religion. Despite negativity, the gospel was preached and care was given. But by the middle of the twentieth century some commenters said that missionary efforts in China had failed.

Then the Chinese Communist Party came to power and expelled foreign missionaries. Soon after, the exodus of foreigners the Chinese Cultural Revolution spread through the country. Organized religion was banned. Temples, pagodas, mosques, and churches were destroyed. Millions of Chinese people starved and died during industrialization efforts that were part of the Great Leap Forward. The message of mercy and compassion seemed like it would be lost in a stripped down, post-religious society.

But the church was not gone, and it was not sleeping. The years have shown that Christianity is now and forever planted in Chinese soil. Tens of millions of Chinese people have embraced the message of the gospel and are choosing a Christ-centered life in spite of opposition. Thousands more convert every day, and if the growth stays at least steady for the next decade, there will be more Christians in China than any other country in the world.[3]

Within these Chinese Christian communities there are efforts to continue the preach and heal model of ministry. Chinese believers are finding innovative ways to share the gospel message and show the love of Christ. Some of this care and compassion is being directed toward orphans, people with disabilities, and people with communicable diseases. These Christians' works do not go unnoticed. Their actions and words move out into the society, forcing unbelievers to question their perception and treatment of these marginalized groups. Chinese Christians are proof that changed people create changed communities.

The aim of this chapter is to remind readers of what God has to say regarding justice for marginalized communities, and through personal accounts, show the strengths and weaknesses of Chinese believers' care for these people. From a foreigner's perspective, I want to show that there are ways in which we

---

Duncan Adams published in two parts through Lexington Theological Seminary.

2. Jesus modeled this preach and heal tactic, and he directed his followers to do the same (Matt. 10:7–8).

3. Stark and Wang, *A Star in the East*, 2.

can encourage, support, and equip Chinese believers' ministries of mercy and compassion. With any discussion regarding China, there are few absolutes. China is massive and diverse. East Asian culture is dynamic and complex. These thoughts are humbly submitted with the confidence that Christ's gospel and compassion will forever be cross-cultural and life changing.

Biblical Justice for the Marginalized

The Bible shows us that God cares about people. And not just their physical well-being. He also cares about their social standing. While everyone possesses equal worth as an image bearer of God, the sinfulness of man perpetually pushes people to the margins of society. The rich take advantage of the poor, and the strong look down on the weak. When faced with the reality of marginalized life, people are quick to call it wrong, unfair, or unjust, but few people offer solutions. There are no simple solutions for restoring the status of marginalized people groups.

In the Old Testament, God calls people out of the chaotic world so that he might establish something ordered and unique. God told Abraham that one part of his calling was to teach his family the way of the Lord, by doing righteousness and justice (Gen. 18:19). The word "righteousness" is a biblical word that is often misunderstood. One might casually define it as "doing what is right all the time." The Bible's usage of righteousness, however, is not just about our actions toward a set of rules. Rather, "righteousness" refers to a perpetual condition of right living, decency, and fairness that people exhibit towards everyone around them. Righteous people will respond to everyone in this way simply because everyone is made in the image of God and possesses equal worth. God's command to Abraham, then, was for him to live an exemplary life, teaching his family through his just treatment of others.

"Justice" is another word that needs to be understood in its Biblical context. Justice is most often practiced through retributive means in which everyone is held to a certain standard and those who fail to live up to this standard are punished for their crimes. But the Bible uses the word justice most often for restoration not retribution. Those who are wrongfully harmed are restored in their relationships and possessions. With these two views of righteousness and justice in hand, Jesus challenges his followers to pursue selfless lives with everyone around them, while also teaching others through treating people with respect and righting visible wrongs.

In the midst of so much evil in the Old Testament, God is often the one who must show restorative justice. When the people of God are being oppressed and wronged by Pharaoh, it is God who steps in to show restorative justice by rescuing the people from Egypt. Tragically, the Israelites ignore God's example once they are in their own land, and they are quickly held to account for their failure to care for the poor and needy by being removed from their country.

In Israel, widows, orphans, immigrants, and the poor composed a unique layer of society to which God had assigned specific laws regarding their care and respect. In Deuteronomy 24, God gives a restriction to not oppress these types of people, and he gives a command to act on their behalf by showing acts of mercy to them. A faithful Israelite could not claim faithfulness to God by simply refraining from further discrimination. They were required to extend compassion.

In the New Testament, Jesus' ministry reveals that many of the poor and outcast in society were the sick and disabled. Jesus made a point to recognize the marginalized, affirm their faith, and forgive their sins. He touched the untouchable and befriended the outcast. He restored their health and their position in society, while at the same time calling them to faith and repentance. Through Jesus' atoning work, believers were able to begin living out the implications of their new righteousness.

When the work of the church began, Christians modeled the care of Jesus towards people, with particular provision given to those now within the church. The book of Acts records how the widows were fed daily, and charitable gifts were taken up for the poor among them. Despite intense persecution, followers of Christ lived a counter-cultural life. That is what Jesus had taught them to do, and the indwelling of the Spirit created a compulsion to pursue evangelism and restoration for everyone around them. The message of the gospel and the actions of Christians proved that the ministry of Jesus was still moving forward. Those on the fringes of society found value, acceptance, and provision through the church. In an anonymous *Letter to Diognetus*, possibly dating from the second century, it was said of Christians:

> "They live in their own native lands, but as aliens; as citizens, they share all things with others; but like aliens, suffer all things. Every foreign country is to them as their native country, and every native land as a foreign country. They marry and have children just like everyone else, but they do not kill unwanted babies. They offer a shared table but not a shared bed. . .They obey appointed laws, and go beyond the laws in their own lives. They love everyone, but are persecuted by all."[4]

---

4. Dowley, Briggs, Linder, and Wright, *Introduction to the History of Christianity*, 67.

Jesus did not teach his disciples to practice justice and mercy in order to transform the entire world into a Christian society. Selfish, power-hungry people will always marginalize the poor and weak. National and global efforts have been trying to tackle problems related to poverty, abandoned children, and disease for years with little positive change. But when Christians care for orphans, they are pointing to a time when the fatherless will see their Heavenly Father. When Christians care for people with disabilities, they are pointing to a time when crying, pain, and grief will pass away. When Christians care for those dying from communicable disease, they are pointing to a time when death will no longer exist. The church's efforts towards these groups are merely shadows of true justice, mercy, and salvation.

While justice and mercy were never intended as an evangelism strategy, when they are visible in the Christian life it spotlights the failures of fallen society and the wisdom of a Christ-centered life. While there are different views on the priority of justice and mercy in Christian ministry, when these needs are near, the Christian response is clear. When Christians care for the marginalized, they obey the command of Jesus to "let your light shine before others, so that they may see your good works and give glory to your Father in heaven" (Matt. 5:16).

Orphans

> "For I rescued the poor who cried out for help, and the fatherless child who had no one to support him." (Job 29:12, CSB)

Problem

The first time that I visited a Chinese orphanage was in 2010. We met up with a small group of other foreigners outside a nondescript four-story building and were soon led upstairs to a room filled with beds. There were twenty to thirty babies in the room all under two years old. For the next two hours we held and fed these children. Most were abandoned at birth. Some had birth defects and most had developmental delays. There were three Chinese women responsible for these babies full-time. Overall it was a positive experience, but I was overwhelmed by one thought — this was only one room.

In this building there were other rooms. Not only other rooms just like this one, but also rooms with children who we were not allowed to be visited because of their behavioral issues. Rooms with children in need of routine physical therapy and education. Rooms with children who had never known the comfort of a family living room or the affirmation of loving parents. In this city of sixteen million people, there were other orphanages. In this country of one billion people, there were countless rooms like this one. These children, because of their situation, were never going to have the same opportunities in their life that my children would.

My wife and I knew that we could never fix a problem this big, but the reality of these children and their needs followed us home. It forced a question into our lives — what is the Christian response to the needs of these children? God brought a period of growth in our lives. Through the Bible, we saw God's commands for the care of the marginalized and forgotten. Through faithful believers, we saw Christ-like examples of orphan care and advocacy. When we moved to China a few years later, we knew that we would be involved in orphan care.

The orphanage in our city was very good and there were several ways for foreigners to be involved with the children there. After living in China for about six months, we welcomed a healthy little girl into our home while she waited for her international adoption to be finalized. A few years later, we took in another little girl who eventually was adopted locally by a Chinese family. Having these children in our home provided many opportunities to talk with people about our Christian understanding of love, parenting, and even marriage. During our time in China, we learned a great deal about adoption and orphan care, and we saw some of the ways that the church is responding to these needs.

Response

Many believers in the church are recognizing that foster care is a clear way to show compassion for orphans. Most of the children in Chinese orphanages have some type of special need, making the personal attention of foster care an even greater need. No matter how good an orphanage may be, a home and a family is better for a child's care and development. Anyone who has participated in foster care knows that it comes with its own unique challenges. Chinese foster care programs and Christian foster families are in need of experienced social workers who are willing to educate them in trauma care, forming attachments, normalization, and community integration. The government is supportive of Chinese foster care programs and some monetary compensation is available.[5]

---

5. Interestingly, some of the local foster families in our city were from the Chinese Muslim communities, either Hui or Salar. There are likely three reasons for this: (1) these ethnic minorities were not limited by the one-child policy so they were

Adoption advocacy is the task of pleading and pursuing the cause of children waiting to be adopted, and it is another way that believers can help these children. Some adoption agencies provide opportunities for volunteers to meet and interact with children in an orphanage with the goal of sharing what they learn about these children. Advocates are able to articulate the needs and personality traits of these children so that potential families are better informed about the children's needs and personalities.

Many of the children who are institutionalized in China have disabilities and developmental delays that they need help overcoming. There are some Christian run facilities and community projects aimed at meeting these needs. Initiatives which provide pediatric physical therapy are attractive partnerships not only for foreigners but also for the government. Foreign partnerships might range in scope from funding, staffing, professional training, and strategic consulting, while partnerships with the government are typically limited to funding. Pediatric physical therapy can create space for more people, believers and unbelievers, to be involved in these children's lives.

One of the greatest acts of love believers can make toward these children is to accept them permanently into their family. While international adoption in China has been happening for years, local adoption by Chinese families has been uncommon. Some of this stems from China's one-child policy that requires parents to pay a lot of money to register additional children. But cultural pressure, particularly from family, seems to be the biggest hindrance. More couples are shifting their perception of adoption, though, and China is now pushing for families to have a second child. The time is right for an adoption movement in China, and Christians should make every effort to lead by example. On the Christian response to adoption, Russell Moore says, "When we adopt—and when we encourage a culture of adoption in our churches and communities—we're picturing something that's true about our God."[6] The church in China has a great opportunity to show their country the God that they serve by making orphans a priority.

People with Disabilities

> "But Peter said, "I don't have silver or gold, but what I do have, I give you: In the name of Jesus Christ of Nazareth, get up and walk!" Then, taking him by the right hand he raised him up, and at once his feet and ankles became strong. So he jumped up and

---

accustomed to having larger families, (2) these groups were typically poorer, and they wanted the monetary compensation, and (3) religious commands to care for orphans.

6. Moore, *Adopted for Life*, 73.

started to walk, and he entered the temple with them—walking, leaping, and praising God." (Acts 3:6–8, CSB)

Problem

As recently as 1980, people with disabilities in China were referred to as *canfei* — "useless people" or "garbage people." They had few rights, and little consideration was being given to changing their situation. Today *canji ren*, "persons with disabilities," is commonly and officially used. While social status and living conditions have improved, the majority of people with disabilities in China still live in poverty. They must rely on the generosity of family or beg for money on the streets.

While we were living in China, we cared for a boy who had to use a wheelchair. I remember a trip to the zoo that was particularly challenging with bus rides, steep paths, and broken sidewalks. In our expat community, there were families who had adopted children with disabilities. One boy and his chair had to be carried up four flights of stairs everyday in order to get to his classroom at school.

In China, there is a significant lack of handicap accessible buildings and public transportation. While new buildings have handicap accessibility requirements, renovations of older buildings are not held to the same standard. Sidewalks and pedestrian walkways are often inaccessible, improperly aligned, and too steep for independent wheel chair use. Even homes in rural areas prove inaccessible because of traditionally high thresholds. Most people have given no thought to the accessibility needs of people with disabilities, and they do not realize how much accessibility can help people with disabilities.

As health care provision in China shifts from government funded to market controlled, poor, unemployed people with disabilities are being left behind. They lack the financial means and availability of medical devices and rehabilitation that they need. Many children born with malformations are able to overcome their disabilities if they have access to the proper braces that are adjusted as the child grows. Unfortunately, these kinds of devices are rarely available or affordable. Rehabilitation facilities and trained physical therapists are also in short supply.

School age children with disabilities face the challenge of attending school. A large percentage drop out or never attend. Even though Chinese law requires that students with disabilities must be accepted, schools lack handicap accessibility, and teachers are not specially trained to handle disabilities. More often, students are rejected from attending a school because the other parents do not want their children in the same classroom as children with disabilities. Special education schools are available in China, but their ability to help the large number of children with disabilities is inadequate.

Any student with disabilities who overcomes primary education faces more barriers at the university level. Government policy in China requires students to pass a physical examination and other policies allow for rejection of applicants with few questions asked. In an effort to deter students with disabilities, some universities have even set higher entrance standards for candidates with disabilities than for normal candidates.[7]

Response

Christians must be the first to reject cultural stereotypes toward people with disabilities. It is shameful that many people living with disabilities are told that it is because of moral failure on their part or their family's. Christians must not merely think of how to do work among these people, but they must also recognize and affirm the place of people with disabilities within the church as a vital part of the Body of Christ.

The Chinese church should seek to identify what disabilities they see in their community and city. This is challenging because of the stigma surrounding disabilities. Someone may never mention a homebound relative, and independent people with disabilities may choose to remain homebound as well. Often, in crowded market streets, one can see beggars with severe disabilities, but believers will have to make an effort to identify real needs over organized panhandling. There are a great number of children in Chinese orphanages living with disabilities who could use the love and attention of Christians.

Pediatricians say that 6 percent of all children worldwide are born with a serious birth defect. With China's high population, the need for rehabilitation workers is even more pronounced. Similarly, people who suffer serious accidents, partial paralysis, or stroke are also in need of these same rehab services that are severely limited in eastern Asia.[8]

Many people living with disabilities can receive improved quality of life with strict physical therapy. Depending on the disability, treatments can be very simple and are easily taught to volunteers. Specialists are typically needed to assess and diagnosis someone's needs, but a volunteer rehab technician can perform the needed therapy. These rehab technicians could also teach family members how to perform the daily therapy.

7. Y-Wang, "A Glance at People with Disabilities in China."
8. Fielding, *Preach and Heal,* 135.

There was a baby girl who was abandoned in our city. When she was found, her muscles were very stiff so she was listed as a special needs child. After several months in a foster family in which she was receiving range of motion therapy, all of her muscles had relaxed, and she was moved to the healthy child list.

When believers intentionally enter into these situations, they are coming to the aid of caregivers who are exhausted and desperate for help. And from the moment they enter these peoples' lives they are bringing respect, compassion, and courage. And unlike other practices that are "hands-off," physical therapy is completely "hands-on." With rehabilitation, Christians can provide routine, therapeutic physical touch to these people.

Many people with physical disabilities will learn some sort of independence, but their ability to earn income is limited. In China, there are government entities that help individuals with specific disabilities to learn a trade. For example, it is common for people living with blindness to learn massage. But there are plenty of other jobs that people with disabilities are capable of handling. But it requires small business owners to choose someone who is disabled over someone who is able bodies. It requires some to establish more work programs and opportunities for people with disabilities. Why can the church not be the leader in this area?

HIV/AIDS

> "Right away a man with leprosy came up and knelt before him, saying, "Lord, if you are willing, you can make me clean." Reaching out his hand, *Jesus touched him*, saying, "I am willing; be made clean." Immediately his leprosy was cleansed."
> (Matthew 8:2–3, CSB)

Problem

Human Immunodeficiency Virus (HIV), the microbe that causes Acquired Immunodeficiency Syndrome (AIDS), has been a growing problem in China for only a few decades. HIV is the fourth leading cause of death worldwide. Millions are infected, including many believers in the church, and millions of children are orphaned by AIDS. Perhaps no other disease is as well known or feared.

Many of the stories surrounding HIV/AIDS in China are alarming. Family members fearing contamination may forcibly quarantine sick individuals and provide limited food and care. In some orphanages, staff may keep HIV+ children in isolation with meager care or comfort. Hospitals may deny care entirely, limiting healthcare options. Local offices tasked with monitoring cases and adjusting medicines are understaffed and not utilized properly. Children may be abandoned by their family and community and grow up alone on the streets.

Before moving to Asia, I had not thought much about HIV. I remember hearing people talk fearfully about the risks of transmission, and that there was no cure. When Christian workers from another city in China started reaching out to find medical care and short-term housing for a severely sick HIV+ teenager named Ben. We felt compelled to help, but we did not know where to start.

Because of HIV, local hospitals were not admitting him, and the county hospitals were ill equipped to treat him. Our home was a good fit, because my wife is a nurse and there was an infectious doctor in our city who was willing to help us treat Ben. We started planning to bring him to our city, and then the doctor and I travelled to pick him up.

When I first met Ben, he was staying in the last room on an empty hall of an old hospital. Few people came to see him other than the girl responsible for bringing him meals. He had developed frostbite that winter and poor nutrition had left him emaciated. As far as we knew, his HIV medications had not been adjusted in years, and he was not expected to ever leave that room.

After only being in our home for a few hours, Ben had to be admitted to the hospital. He was so sick that we were not positive he would make it through the night. Patient care in Chinese hospitals is largely dependent on round the clock assistance from friends and family. Doctors are only seen in their offices. Nurses only give medicine and record vital signs. Because of this, we were in desperate need of people to sit with Ben when we could not be there. We had no idea if anyone would want to help. The calls went out, and the church came to Ben's bedside. Christian expats we barely knew. Chinese brothers and sisters we had never met before. Christ-like mercy and compassion are what fueled long nights with Ben, helped him use the bathroom, fed him food, and showed him love. After five nights in the hospital he came back to our house, and we saw him smile for the first time.

Believers continued to play a huge role in his recovery. He had a Christian counselor that he met with regularly to talk through his feelings in ways that we were not equipped. Our Chinese tutor began to work on his reading, writing, and math, all of which had been neglected by being in the hospital. Another believer helped cook food he really enjoyed so that he would gain more weight. After two and a half months in our home, he went to live at a group foster home for HIV+ children run by believers.

Response

Ben said that his biological parents died, and he was left at the boarding school when he was three years old. He did not remember his mother or father. He had no family that claimed relation to him. Many of the other children at his old boarding school were called orphans, but they had extended family that they would visit on holidays. Because of the stigma of HIV in Asia many families are not willing to take care of the children. When Ben lived with us, we never told a single local person about his disease. Our landlords could have evicted us. Our local friends could have abandoned us. Coworkers could have shunned us. For his protection, we told no one. They knew he was very sick, but we never named his disease. Because we chose not to tell people, they would come into our home, sit with him, and touch and hug him.

The church of Jesus Christ is called to show deep love and compassion to everyone, including those infected and affected by HIV/AIDS. Christians should be at the forefront of restoring life and dignity to these people. Jesus' teaching, his example, and the transformative power of the cross are central in a holistic gospel response to these needs. Believers must be quick to denounce any discrimination, hostility, and condemnation towards those living with this disease. These things are sinful and discredit the body of Christ. After all, everyone has fallen short of the glory of God and is in need of the same grace. Believers must realize that many are infected through no fault of their own, and sometimes it occurred by simply caring for others.[9]

There are many Chinese believers who are pushing back against societal discrimination of those infected with communicable diseases. They have seen the servanthood and acceptance modeled by Jesus, and they are risking their reputations to care for these marginalized groups. The church's respect for these people will not go unnoticed.

While there is no cure for HIV/AIDS, treatment has improved to the point that regular testing and medication can reduce viral levels to the point that they are not transmissible. Positive individuals can even get married and have children with extremely low likelihood of transmission. If every person infected with HIV could be identified, educated, and medicated, then there would be considerable progress made towards containing the

---

9. In some regions of China, the virus was spread through villages and counties because of a predatory blood economy. Villages were asked to sell their blood at government blood stations, and in return, they would become rich. When blood stations were not available, individuals would go door-to-door and solicit blood donations, and then sell the blood to government entities. Lack of knowledge, training, and sterilization spread disease to everyone.

virus. Unfortunately, this goal is not very practical and may be an infringement on privacy. But there are two groups that can be helped by the church: (1) those in need of care and (2) those in need of education.

The first group is more challenging because HIV and AIDS patients do not want to self-identify. If there are partnerships with local doctors, Christian teams could make regular visits to patients' homes and hospital rooms. These visits could be used to assure that the patient is taking all of their medication on schedule, could give counseling, and provide palliative care in later stages if no one else is available.

The second group of people can be helped through community development programs. Since there are already initiatives like this being conducted by non-profit organizations and government programs, Christian teams could accompany these workers as they visit homes to teach about HIV prevention. These efforts will look very different in larger cities than in smaller villages.

Christian teams should seek training from trained physicians so that they are able to identify and treat basic symptoms of AIDS, like fever, rashes, and pain. These counseling and education initiatives are not just for patients. The entire family is being affected by this disease, and they need attention.

Because children with communicable diseases are not allowed to attend normal schools, believers have an opportunity to care through academics. There are schools like this in China, but most have no Christian presence. These children will also have a hard time ever getting work or attending a university because of their disease. Many Christians are small business owners, and they can offer jobs or apprenticeships to equip these kids for the future.

Thankfully, there are some Christian groups engaging in all of these methods of care and education. One good example is a Christian run group foster home for HIV+ children. The staff care for the children living with them, ensuring they receive their medication and testing. But they also care for many other families in the community who have HIV+ children. The workers visit the homes, take children to appointments at the hospital, make sure medication is administered properly, and educate family members. As these kids get older, they not only need help getting and education and finding a job, but also knowing how to manage their disease and navigating the hospital system. The church must learn to play a vital role in all stages of HIV+ peoples' lives.

Conclusion

The Church in China is proving itself to be just like those apple trees that still grow in Kham Tibet. While foreign at first, God has made the gospel take root in China, and it continues to be fruitful long after the initial planters are gone.

China's rapid urban growth is steadily stretching the budgets of social services while at the same time compounding social needs. Even as Christians in China face increased opposition from government policies, they have a unique role to play in caring for people who are being isolated by these changes.

Foreigners wishing to participate in this movement of God in China should consider their ministries first. Are their churches and denominations leading by example with regard to marginalized groups in their own communities? Is care being shown to teen moms, addicts, and the poor? Is the church a place of inclusion for these groups?

The Chinese church is very evangelistic, but it is not just the message of the gospel that is on the move. Yes, the message of the gospel is changing hearts, but it is also the acts of love and Biblical justice that are providing visible context for the message. God is using these communities of faith to transform pockets of Chinese society in small but significant ways. Compassion and mercy are powerful tools in the hands of Spirit filled Christ followers.

PART III

Impacting Chinese House Churches

Chapter 7

Missionaries reaching Chinese theologically

(especially through seminaries)

ALLEN YEH

Prospectus: China, being one of the two 'centers' (along with sub-Saharan Africa) of world Christianity today, has a remarkable role to play, not only in being a receiver of missions but also a sender of missions. The way that seminaries interface with this dynamic is critical, as they can be a force for centripetal mission (drawing Chinese toward themselves in order to go back to the Chinese) as well as centrifugal mission (training Westerners to minister in China), but the current state is untenable and a complete 'rethink' of the purposes and structure of theological education is needed in light of the changing demographic and center of Christianity in the world today.

When people think of missions, they do not often think about seminaries. This is ironic, because one of the three main verbs in the Great Commission—along with "make disciples" and "baptize"—is "teach." But often the teaching is thought of simply as evangelism. However, evangelism is merely the initiatory act of teaching, to compel someone to believe that Jesus is Lord, and of his propitiatory sacrificial act on the cross on behalf of all mankind to all who would have faith in him. However, teaching extends far beyond that, to a more robust and deeper understanding of the knowledge of God. This kind of theological education can take the form of lifelong learning from: 1) a local church (in sermons and Sunday schools or Bible studies), or 2) from parachurch organizations on secular campuses (e.g. Campus Crusade for Christ, InterVarsity Christian Fellowship, etc.), or 3) in a formal degree program such as a BD (Bachelor of Divinity), MDiv (Master of Divinity), or even a DMin (Doctor of Ministry, for practitioners) or PhD (Doctor of Philosophy, for academics). This chapter will address the last option mentioned, and in the unique context of China.

THE RATIONALE FOR SEMINARIES IN THE MAJORITY WORLD

The phenomenon of World Christianity—the shift of the center of gravity of Christianity to the Majority World aka Two Thirds World in the last fifty years or so—has dramatically changed the landscape of Christianity worldwide. Instead of most of the Christians being located in the West, the average Christian today is to be found in Africa, Asia, Latin America, the Middle East, the Pacific, the Caribbean, and any number of non-"traditional" spots for Christianity. Actually, it is ironic because the ancient "traditional" spots where the church originated *were* places like Ethiopia, Turkey, and India— so actually Europe is the foreign soil rather than Africa, the Middle East, or Asia. So, in essence, this is a reformation (a return to the roots) rather than a new phenomenon.

There are many ramifications to this back-to-the-roots landscape of Christianity, such as:

- The majority of the Christians in the world are not in the West, but the majority of the power, wealth, and influence (like publishing houses) remain in the West. This is actually a return to the form of the early church, where the majority of Christians were not the ones with power but were the persecuted poor minorities. Perhaps this creates a more authentic type of Christianity today, one which is more communal (rather than individualistic) and one which understands what real suffering is.

- Missionaries are going from everywhere to everywhere, often with great effect. For example, a brown-skinned South American can go to the Middle East and "blend in" physiologically, and also without any of the negative political baggage that a white Westerner might carry with them. Or, the Chinese can do missions "back to Jerusalem" across the Silk Road, because Central Asians likewise do not have any problems politically with the Chinese whereas they may with white Westerners.

- Worldviews are changing. Pentecostalism is the fastest-growing form of Christianity around the world, and the resulting pneumatology will become a new way of framing Christian theology. Also, modernism and postmodernism (Western post-Enlightenment ways of thinking) are now being mixed with premodernism, which is more in line with how the ancient Christians viewed the world, with an openness to the supernatural and a Middle Tier of reality (unlike Westerns who have an "excluded middle").
- The average Christian is increasingly female, and young. The hegemony of older males no longer represents the common face of Christianity around the world.

However, in addition to all of the above, the task of Western missionaries is changing. If Christians in the Two Thirds World constitute the majority of numbers in the global church, then evangelism is no longer the primary missionary endeavor of Westerners. If the local people know the language and culture better than Westerners do, it seems highly nonsensical (not to mention financially inefficient) to get a Western missionary to raise thousands of dollars to fly to that other country and learn the language to preach the Gospel. For that amount of money, many more indigenous people could be supported who already know the target audience to do the evangelism, so it would be faster and cheaper.

So, does this mean we call a moratorium on missions? No, because the goal is not separation of the West and the Majority World, the goal is still unity through partnership. Therefore, the task of Westerners should be more to disciple, empower, and resource the Majority World, rather than to simply evangelize them. However, partnership implies moving away from paternalism toward actual sharing. But sharing means mutuality even amidst differences. In other words, if the Western world has more money and books but the Majority World has more people, then the Western world can support the Majority World with money and books, and the Majority World can supply the Western world with manpower in the form of more workers in the mission field.

However, it is not quite that neat, because there is a very fine line in navigating the issue of paternalism. Because imagine if the Western world decides that they will stop sending evangelists to the Majority World but will just ship loads of their books to them instead—the power still remains with the West because the formation of theological ideas still is in Western form, and it will continue to remain with the West as long as the money, the publishing houses, and the seminaries remain with the West.

How do we overcome this disparity? Because the goal is for indigenous churches to move beyond the three selves (not to be confused with the Three Self Patriotic Movement, or TSPM, churches which is the official governmental church of mainland China) of self-governing, self-propagating, and self-sustaining, toward the fourth self: self-theologizing. In the Africa Bible Commentary, the authors (all indigenous Africans) characterized the state of Christianity in Africa as being "a mile wide and an inch deep." This led them to write the aforementioned commentary, to create a grand work of self-theologizing, instead of simply mimicking Western theology. So, how do we get to that place? Let us work backward:

- In order to have proper self-theologizing, you need educated theologians with PhDs in biblical theology and systematic theology who can write many books, and publishing houses that can print and distribute these books widely. (But in this chapter, we will not deal with the publishing houses, as the focus is on seminaries).

- In order to have enough educated theologians, you need Christians smart enough and hard-working enough and willing to pursue a degree program. The Majority World certainly has plenty of those. But they often do not have the financial resources to go overseas.

- Here is where the Western world comes in: one option is that Westerners can give a lot of money to fund the Majority World PhD candidates to get their degree in the West (like John Stott did with his Langham Scholarships). But, although it is good for the few who are lucky enough to receive it, this is highly ineffective cost-wise (each student will require airfare, food and lodging, and tuition expenses), similar to how cost-ineffective it is to send a Western missionary to the Majority World. And, Majority World students would often have to operate in a foreign language, English. So, the better option is that Westerns would give a lot of money to build theological seminaries and universities in the Majority World, thus enabling Majority World students to stay local and conduct their studies in their own language and culture and context.

- However, in order to have Majority World seminaries and universities get accreditation and credibility, there need to be enough professors holding PhDs to ensure quality of academic scholarship. The Majority World often does not have enough (yet) to staff their own seminaries, even though their student body may be huge. The West, however, has the opposite problem: the market is glutted with holders of the PhD degree but who lack jobs because there are not enough positions available. The solution seems simple: Westerners ought to teach overseas and fill those positions (there is also an ironic acknowledgment of many Westerners unwilling to do so due to not enough financial compensation, so they would rather stay in the West and not use their PhD than to use it overseas for a small salary or to fund-raise for it). But the question remains: how do we guard against paternalism, where the Westerners are all the teachers with all the ideas, and the Majority World are the students who have to imbibe all they are taught? This is why self-theologizing is so important. Eventually, as more Majority World Christians are educated, they can learn to think for themselves, and go beyond the Western curriculum they are taught and be able to apply theology to their own situations and contexts and in words they understand and are more comfortable with. The goal is for Majority World PhD holders to teach in their own contexts (there is also an ironic acknowledgment that many Majority World students who study in the West decline to return home to their native contexts for various reasons, thus creating a brain drain), as well as for some to teach in Western contexts to educate Westerners.

- There is a final piece of the puzzle: prestige of institution. Numbers do not necessarily make for influence. Imagine if we see a day where there are more theological seminaries and universities in the Majority World to serve all those Christians. But the minority from the West will still have the voices if they graduate from places like Oxford, Edinburgh, or Yale. So, having some Majority World students receive their PhDs in prestigious Western institutions is still necessary to some degree, to build up that institution's prestige. And, over time, that institution will be able to stand on its own credibility.

Admittedly, this is a "long game." We will not see results in this generation, but it may take several generations for this to bear fruit.

TYPES OF SEMINARIES IN CHINA AND GREATER ASIA

How does China fit the above-stated paradigm? What are the unique challenges or opportunities for China in the world of theological education?

For the uninitiated, they may be surprised that mainland China allows Christianity, or churches, or even theological seminaries. Although these need to follow certain strictures in order to not be breaking the law, they are legitimate institutions and have their own long history. These seminaries all fall under the auspices and authority of the China Christian Council (CCC), the State Administration for Religious Affairs (SARA), and the Three-Self Patriotic Movement (TSPM). However, some people feel like their freedoms of speech and action are curtailed under these offices, which is why they resort to underground house churches or go to overseas institutions of higher learning.

Others to consider would be seminaries within China but located in Special Administrative Regions (SARs) like Hong Kong Baptist University. And further afield, there are those listed under the Association for Theological Education in Southeast Asia (ATESEA) which comprise over one hundred schools in sixteen countries (including China), e.g. Trinity Theological College in Singapore; Asia Pacific Theological Seminary in Baguio City, The Philippines; or Myanmar Institute of Theology in Yangon. Some people may go study at these institutions for more than just freedom of expression, but they may be strategic. For example, being located in Singapore—a largely Christian nation surrounded by Muslim nations—could be fruitful for interreligious dialogue and exchange. Another reason to study at these seminaries in Greater Asia would be for language issues, in case someone wanted to do their degree in English (as offered in Singapore) or any number of Southeast Asian languages.

One other category to bear in mind are theological seminaries planted by parachurch organizations. For example, Cru (formerly Campus Crusade for Christ) has started many seminaries in the Majority World, although most of them—four—are in Africa. Two, however, are in Asia, and they include East Asia School of Theology (EAST) in Singapore, and International Graduate School of Leadership in Manila, The Philippines. There is also one in the Middle East, and one in Eastern Europe. It is appreciated that Africa, which is far poorer than Asia, has been a source of greater focus for Cru. However, Asia has a far greater population than Africa and also needs to be served with regard to their numbers. And just as with churches, the four-self model should be the eventual goal: for the indigenous seminaries to become self-governing, self-propagating, self-supporting, and self-theologizing. Ironically, China—being more "closed" to the outside world than democratic countries—has more national autonomy than many other Majority World countries, by sheer virtue of the fact that they already run their own churches, they do not have as much Western influence in terms of theological ideas, and their economy has grown to first-world standards in many respects so they are not as under-resourced financially as churches in many other countries.

One final note: a major limitation of many seminaries in the Majority World is that many of them only offer Bachelor degrees and not Masters degrees. This is especially true in Latin America, but also somewhat in Africa and Asia. One of the reasons for this is that, if an undergraduate degree is expected as a prerequisite for seminary (as in the United States, to fulfill Association of Theological Schools, or ATS, accreditation), many Majority World people could not fulfill that requirement because it is a high bar. But if seminaries offer baccalaureate-level education, that makes them far more accessible to the common layperson. However, this presents a difficulty, because if the ultimate goal is to train up many seminarians to PhD level so they can train their own people (a Master's degree is sufficient to practice ministry, but a PhD is required to teach and to write new theology), many people can achieve entry-level education but not many people can attain the highest level necessary to be a four-self church.

Publishing houses—while not the focus of this chapter—deserve a mention at this point. China—unlike many Majority World countries—actually has the resources to publish, as Amity Publisher in Nanjing is actually the largest Bible publisher in the entire world! However, they are all in-country publishers (i.e. these books never reach the West). If Western publishers like Zondervan can get the permission to publish them in the U.S. and abroad, then the global distribution can happen.

WAYS TO GET INVOLVED WITH SEMINARIES IN CHINA

There are at least four different ways that one may become involved with seminaries in China. The first two suggestions are for native Chinese, and the last two are for foreigners:

1. For native Chinese: teach there, but this requires you getting a PhD first. I realize there is a tendency in Asia (and in much of the Majority World) to value practical ministry over academia. In the Western world, the tendency is the opposite, which is why there are so many more academics from the West. But the imbalance needs to be addressed. While undoubtedly the focus on missions and pastoral ministry is necessary and amazingly encouraging that there are so many workers in the harvest field, there is more than one way to serve God's Kingdom. An army needs not only infantry but commanders and generals. Therefore, missionaries need to be trained by faculty before they are sent out. Do not underestimate the value of years of study. Even Jesus studied for a long time. He only did his public ministry from ages 30–33; but what was he doing prior to age 30? He was preparing, "growing in wisdom and stature and in favor with God and man" (Luke 2:52) and later being trained as a rabbi after first having had a job as a carpenter. Even when he was about to start his public ministry, he still had to prepare himself further by fasting in the wilderness

for 40 days. And the Twelve started off as disciples ("students") before they became apostles ("sent-out" missionaries). They had to study for three years under the tutelage of the Master Teacher, Jesus himself, before they were able to be unleashed on the world. And Jesus left them, encouraging them to do even greater things than he did in the power of the Holy Spirit. This did not only include miracles and preaching, but the Apostles' teaching (Acts 2:42) which became the foundational theological bedrock for the Church. I know there will be times during the PhD process when you will question the usefulness of the process, and the time and money and energy required to accomplish this. But getting a PhD is the gift that keeps on giving. If you are a Majority World theologian with a legitimate PhD, you will be given so many platforms to speak and write worldwide. And, like missionary Robert Morrison (the first Protestant missionary to China), you can accomplish even more after you have passed on than while you were alive by virtue of the writings you leave behind.

2. For native Chinese: minister there. There are two types of mission: centrifugal (going outward) and centripetal (drawing inward). The former type is the New Testament model, as the Holy Spirit sent out apostles all over the world. The latter type is the Old Testament model, drawing people in by virtue of attraction. This is what Israel was called to do, to be a "light to the nations" (Isaiah 49:6). Universities work on the centripetal model. If people are drawn from overseas to study in Chinese seminaries, being an on-campus chaplain or minister can be a great advantage, where you do not even need to go overseas to reach the nations. Of course, people coming to Christian seminaries and universities would most likely be Christian already (thus the care for them would be pastoral); but people coming to Chinese secular universities would largely not be Christians, and they can be reached missionally by being exposed to the Gospel through classes. So, I would encourage Chinese who get PhDs to not only consider PhDs in theology and Bible, but also in other fields such as STEM (Science, Technology, Engineering, and Mathematics), humanities, and social sciences. The philosophy of Christian education is integration, where "all truth is God's truth." Therefore, sometimes it is of greater effectiveness to reach someone via being great at a "secular" subject than reaching someone using Christian theology or evangelism. Historical and contemporary examples include: Isaac Newton, Jeremy Lin, J.R.R. Tolkien, Roberto Clemente, Francis Collins, Martin Luther King Jr., and Bono, who are the greatest trailblazers of their kind and who all

happened to be Christians. But if you can be the equivalent on university or seminary campuses, you can have an incredible platform to speak to people. This is also why getting a PhD is important, for credibility and respect. But having a PhD *and* being known for a huge contribution to society will surely open many doors.

3. For foreigners: if you have a PhD, teach there. But teach with an eye toward the four-self church, that the eventual goal is for the Chinese to "own" their seminaries themselves. Mao Zedong famously said, "If you give a man a fish, you feed him for a day. But if you teach a man to fish, you feed him for a lifetime." So, teach them theology and practical ministry in ways that enable them to develop life skills to think for themselves rather than simply Western content. Give them a framework, do not simply have them download information. This is trickier than it sounds, because many Asian educational systems are conducted as largely rote memorization. You may even get insistence from the Chinese themselves that that is what they want and need. But do not believe it! Ironically, rote memorization is something that originally Westerners did, whereas Easterners did more of an indirect question-and-answer type of learning (what we often call the "Socratic Method," but obviously it was not just the Greeks who did this—Jesus himself did this too, cf. the Parable of the Good Samaritan when he answered the Teacher of the Law's question with a story and had him answer his own question about the Second Greatest Commandment). For some reason, at one point in history the learning styles flipped and Westerners started valuing "teaching a man to fish" education and Asians started doing more "give a man a fish" education. Chinese need to recover their roots, Confucian-style. Also, Christian education has the philosophy of offering a holistic education. Training someone is not just for training the mind, but also their character, their ethics, their priorities, their desires, and their souls.

4. For foreigners: donate there if you have the resources. Money, books, and buildings are all in short supply. Do not simply donate to Harvard, which already has an embarrassment of riches. But give what you have to the needy and the poor, and "your reward will be great in heaven"! There are other ways to get involved if you are not possessed of great personal wealth, like myself. I serve on the Board of Trustees of the Foundation for Theological Education in Southeast Asia (FTESEA) which actually began as a foundation to support Nanjing Union Theological Seminary but eventually expanded to cover a multitude of theological institutes throughout China and Southeast Asia. Our mission is

to be stewards of a large endowment that was left by a generous couple long ago. We use the interest to disseminate as scholarship money and library funds to seminarians and seminaries throughout Asia.

All told, the future of Majority World seminaries looks bright *if* many of the above ideas are followed. This is not the definitive and exhaustive guide to aiding missionaries and nationals in supporting theological education in China, however. This needs to be a collaborative endeavor where many people think together—foreigners and indigenous Chinese alike—to ensure that theological education in China has depth and not just breadth, and that they can stand on their own two feet without Western support. As such, I hope this chapter serves as a good starting point. And, it is also encouraging that China is well ahead of many seminaries in the Majority World, as they have been operating on the "three-self" principle for a long time, and hopefully their "fourth self" will be made available to the world widely. And perhaps, one day, "the student will become the teacher" as we in the West can learn from our Chinese counterparts more than they are learning from us.

Chapter 8

Missionaries' Role in Theological Education in China

Urban Farmer

INTRODUCTION

Over the past thirty-two years, I have devoted myself to ministering to the church in the Chinese context, specifically to those in and from the People's Republic of China (PRC). For the latter half of this time, I have carried a deep conviction that the church in China has desperately needed well-trained leaders. This conviction eventually led me to consider theological education which then resulted in me co-founding an "open" (or *gongkai* in Chinese), but unregistered seminary in southwest China. The school now serves students from over 20 different provinces and administrative zones throughout the nation.

The challenges are numerous and the task is at times overwhelming but the ministry is immensely fulfilling and desperately needed by the house church in China. In many ways, for me, it is the realization of a dream I have had since I was a young, newly-married seminary student in the late 1990s. My thesis here is to touch on some of the challenges that a seminary like ours faces and hopefully provide a bit of a framework for understanding and implementing theological education under a repressive, atheistic regime. In particular, however, my interest will not only be to look at the challenges of theological education in China but to explore the role of the missionary in helping to answer those challenges. Is there still a need for a missionary presence in China? If so, what kind of needs should missionaries be trying to meet in the church?

Although the scope of this work is focused on a rather narrow subject matter, there is still no shortage of material that could potentially be covered. With this in mind, it becomes necessary to recognize the limitations of space and therefore keep the contents within well-defined boundaries. While many worthy topics and matters could be addressed, we will only concern ourselves with four areas: contextualization, sustainability, partnership and, accreditation.

Definitions

Contextualization is a word that, in the past, was met with a good deal of suspicion by evangelicals, most likely because it had been first promoted by those in the theologically "liberal" camp. Originally the term was developed by Shoki Coe, a Presbyterian minister in a Theological Seminary in southern Taiwan in conjunction with the World Council of Churches. In recent years, however, it has been used more widely by evangelicals especially in the area of missions. One reason, perhaps, for this shift is that contextualization and other related terms (e.g. indigenization, cultural adaptation, etc.) are being defined in different ways than they were in the past. In academic debates these terms are interpreted differently by different scholars and consensus on how to define these terms is allusive. When we use the word contextualization, we do not mean simply "to say what. . . itching ears want to hear" (2 Tim. 4:3, NIV). Instead it aims at answering life's question from a thoroughly biblical perspective.[1] Therefore, this paper will define contextualization as "translating and adapting the communication and ministry of the gospel to a particular culture without compromising the essence and particulars of the gospel itself."[2]

Sustainability focuses on the ability of a theological institution to serve its current constituents as well as future generations by managing its resources wisely. When we use the word sustainability, we need to clearly define what it is that we mean by this term. To that end, we define sustainability as the "ability to meet the needs of the present generation without having to compromise the ability of future generations to meet their own needs."[3]

1. Keller, *Center Church*.
2. Ibid.
3. Bellon, *Leading Financial Sustainability in Theological Institutions*.

The concept of *partnership* aims at defining a philosophy of missions that recognizes and responds to the needs of the local church as defined by their own words, not simply by scholarly analysis or the perspective of those who did *not* grow up in the local culture.

Finally, our discussion of *accreditation* aims at answering the question of how the theological institutions of China go about connecting with the global church. Currently, this is a major factor in issues such as degree recognition and faculty development. Creating a clear pathway for schools outside of China to recognize degrees from house church seminaries is also part of what accreditation aims to accomplish. Once again, given space limitations, we will only focus on house church seminaries.

Presuppositions and Terms

To proceed effectively it will help if we clarify certain presuppositions and terms that will come up frequently throughout this piece. Helpful explanations and definitions will hopefully remove any potential for misunderstanding and make clear what we are trying to accomplish.

Our first presupposition is that our reader knows at least something of the last seventy-five years of Chinese church history in the People's Republic of China (PRC). There is no need for expertise in this field but understanding the basic facts that China is both a repressive, Communist regime promoting a militant form of atheism[4] and at the same time is one of the fastest-growing Protestant churches in the world, is necessary information to establish before moving forward.

Second, we will frequently be referring to the *house church* and not the *underground church*. The reason for this is subtle but important. While on the one hand, these terms are often synonymous when used in contrast to the government-approved, Protestant Three-Self Patriotic Church, the two terms (underground church and house church) describe different aspects and even different kinds of unregistered churches in China. The term house church is used more broadly to describe all unregistered churches who meet either "openly" (*gongkai*) or secretively (*dixia* or underground) and came about because many of these churches began in someone's apartment or house (even though many of them now meet in office buildings or other larger venues). While many are familiar with stories from both past and present of Christians in China meeting in secret locations under a repressive Communist regime there are a growing number of house churches (many of which are urban) that have chosen to intentionally be *gongkai*,

---

4. Yang, *Religion in China*.

They are visible and some even have their names listed in the lobby of the office building where they meet for worship. I have spent the last eight years in China working with a *gongkai* church.

There has been an intense wave of repression unleashed by the Chinese Communist Party (CCP) to drive out these *gongkai* gatherings since new policies were implemented in February of 2018. The net result is that many of these gatherings have, whether through coercion or on their own volition, begun meeting in private homes.

Finally, it is crucial to this discussion to understand that when we speak of "Chinese," we need to be specific. Currently, three very different cultural contexts include people who consider themselves Chinese and who legitimately claim that they live in China: Mainland China, Hong Kong, and Taiwan. I have not even mentioned Macau or the Chinese living outside of China among the diaspora. It does not take very long until we begin to realize that simply referring to Chinese culture or the modern Chinese context can be somewhat confusing. For clarity sake, I will refer to the Mainland Chinese context as PRC, while Taiwan and Hong Kong, I will refer to as such.

Contextualization

Issues related to contextualization and the complexity of understanding what is meant by Chinese culture have been insightfully addressed in some very helpful pieces (Park, 2014; Kwan and Lee, 2010) by exposing overly simplistic definitions, yet it seems that these one-dimensional definitions still prevail even in scholarly circles. Given issues of colonialism, modernization and globalization the lines between traditional and modern need to be understood without equating modern with Western. In a Chinese context like Hong Kong, the fabric of Chinese culture must take seriously the 100–year history of British colonialism that preceded 1997, and which has been woven into the identity of the people. In Taiwan, there was, most recently, a 50–year period of Japanese occupation from 1895 to 1945, which impacted the culture and people in profound ways. Similarly, in the PRC the influence of a Soviet-style of Communism has had a massive impact on the educational and political systems. In both the Hong Kong and PRC context there are significant factors that have shaped the culture that are in sharp contrast to traditional Chinese culture.

One clear example of this in the PRC is the educational system. The centuries-old Imperial Examination system (*keju*) was done away with in the late Qing Dynasty and several decades later replaced with a modern, but foreign education system. That system was eventually replaced by a Soviet, science-centered model of education. This factor plays an enormous role in shaping the mindset and worldview of hundreds of millions of Chinese citizens. This educational system that originated in the Soviet Union (USSR) is used as a tool to mold the young minds of China's citizens throughout their entire educational tenure. Indoctrinating the thinking of millions of PRC citizens, the current education system functions in a way that the previous education system in China was not able to, simply by the fact that it is offered to virtually all of China's citizens.

Contextualization in China, therefore, must address the cultural narratives that are being taught during those formidable years of education. Any approach to contextualize the gospel and theological education in the PRC must take a look at modern Chinese culture and the essential cultural narratives that it promotes.[5]

The modern PRC social narrative consists of several elements including concepts such as nationalism, socialism, and freedom.[6] How these terms are defined, understood and challenged using a biblical worldview must be part of what informs contextualized theological education in the PRC.

Less than one year after our seminary opened in the PRC we quickly realized our Master of Divinity and Bachelor of Divinity students could not think with a comprehensive Christian worldview. There was no doubt in our minds that these students were devout Christians but due to years of Marxist-Leninist education, which embraces militant style of atheism,[7] our students were often unaware of how deeply ingrained the teachings of their atheistic education had influenced their worldview. Even those who grew up in Christian homes (mostly from the countryside) were not properly instructed on how to re-think these cultural narratives. How do I show my loyalty to my country as a Christian? How do I think about politics and economics as a Christian? What does true freedom of conscience mean? These are not easy questions to answer so we eventually decided that our students needed courses in these areas.

To answer these questions from a biblical perspective we designed a curriculum of humanities courses that both our MDiv and BDiv students are required to take. The courses are designed to address the atheistic worldview narrative that our students have been immersed in and give them a redemptive-historical narrative for subjects such as science, philosophy, art, ethics, and law.

---

5. Keller, *Center Church*.
6. Yang, "Cultural Dynamics in China."
7. Yang, *Religion in China*.

This is just one example of how theological education can approach contextualization by addressing the modern cultural narratives that inform people's thinking in the PRC. In addition to providing this contextual element, the PRC house church needs to engage the global church by being conversant in the vocabulary of theological concepts, both systematic and biblical. Hermeneutical issues need to be addressed as well- learning from the lessons of church history and applying gospel truths to the modern context will mean presenting new perspectives that in some ways will be uniquely Chinese but will also contribute to the global ecclesiastical conversation. Deep familiarity with the voices of the past and yet being able to add something new to the global theological discussion is something we aspire toward for our students.

Sustainability

Helping contextualize theological education for the PRC's future house church leaders is one of the important roles missionaries and mission agencies can and should play in the PRC. Historically speaking, establishing theological institutions on the global mission field has been one of the key contributions mission agencies have played. After 1949, the role of theological education and the missionary in the PRC underwent a dramatic change. By 1951, virtually all missionaries were expelled by the CCP of the newly established PRC. From 1966–1979 religion was outlawed in China, and finally in 1982, under Deng Xiaoping, the CCP began to ease up on their tight restrictions against religion, allowing a degree of freedom for the five approved religions in China (Taoism, Buddhism, Islam, Protestant, and Catholic).[8]

Over the last thirty years a very small number of clandestine foreign missionaries have been able to form partnerships with PRC house churches and in some cases have successfully aided in setting up theological training centers and seminaries. It has been my experience over the past decade that the role of the foreign missionary is still valuable but best served when in equal partnership with local churches. We will say more about this in the section on *partnership*.

The challenge of helping these seminaries become sustainable is no small feat. Ironically, the government's approved Three-Self Patriotic Movement Church (TSPM) holds *support* as a priority. This aspect is one of the three "self's" (Self-Governing, Self-Propagating, Self-Supporting) and refers to the TSPM church's ability to distance itself from foreign resources

---

8. Yang, *Religion in China*.

especially funds. There is a value to this that must be acknowledged especially given the history of Chinese churches that grew overly dependent on foreign funding. However, while borrowing these principles from the mission strategy first promoted by missiologists Henry Venn and Rufus Anderson, the CCP re-defined *self-supporting* in such a way that equates it with patriotism by inextricably connecting it with the government. This structure also fed into the cultural narrative of nationalism which further distanced Chinese Christians from the global church community

The question must be asked, therefore, what does sustainability mean in this context? What we mean when we use this term is that the seminary has reliable streams of resources feeding the life of the seminary while maintaining a level of independence that allows it to pursue the mission of the seminary without getting side-tracked by projects that do not contribute to that mission. An example of this would be an instance where a seminary opens a business to provide a revenue stream to foster financial sustainability since most seminaries globally receive less than 50 percent of their revenue from student's tuition. In many cases that revenue source tends to distract from the overall mission of the seminary and lead to unintentional repercussions.

Many house church seminaries boldly face the challenge of becoming self-supporting without any possibility of government funding. More and more house church congregations and networks are seeing the value of theological education and are willing to fund seminaries and training centers in such a way that nurtures partnership but allows seminaries a degree of independence. Pastors of local congregations need to serve on committees that help give direction to these educational institutions.

Seminaries can create boards that consist of both local pastors and foreign missionaries who know the culture and language. These are valuable partnerships where both sides learn from one another and partner together for the work of God's kingdom.

Revenue streams need to be created that allow seminaries to promote sustainable income to fund seminary operations beyond the tuition fees, and donations from the local church. One such possibility is to have the seminary open a bookstore. While this option does not sound very profitable, at least in the Western context, it is quite profitable in China. Christian literature in China is not readily available due to many government restrictions yet the church is in great need of good books. We have found at our seminary that the income made from selling books at a very small profit or even a free-will offering (if the books were donated) gives us a revenue stream that contributes a sizeable amount to our annual budget (up to 25 percent). The scarcity of Christian literature in China makes the Christian bookstore a reasonable revenue stream because our bookstore carries many books that students cannot purchase elsewhere.

It must be recognized that this comes with a significant risk. Recent CCP policies have targeted publishers and bookstores bringing legal charges against those leading these projects. New security measures will need to be put in place to address these risks but the demand for literature is still quite high in the house church.

While there is no perfect model to create revenue sources since every possible scenario comes with the possibility of risk or loss, nonetheless there are reasonable solutions. Other possible revenue streams could be coffee shops, counseling centers or translation services. Whatever the case, the risk factor cannot be eliminated and therefore seminaries need to aim at risk options that match the seminaries ability to manage such risk while simultaneously being willing to step out in faith and trust God for the resources.

Partnership

Many worthy things can and should be said about the role of partnership in theological education. First, there is the necessary partnership between the seminary and the local church. The adage "as the seminary goes, so goes the church" has proven itself to be true many times over. The church and seminary were not intended to function separately without one considering the interests of the other,[9] but so often we see the opposite occurring. Theological education in the PRC lends itself, in many ways, to strengthening that partnership. Personal connections need to be forged between the church and the seminary to form a basis of trust in an environment like the PRC where schools need to be on the lookout for government informants.

Another important partnership is that of the missionary with the local church. This kind of partnership is filled with obstacles and challenges, many of which relate to the ability of both parties (both the missionary and the local church leaders) to understand, communicate and effectively work with one another. In many ways, this is not dissimilar to any other mission field but in the PRC, there is the extra risk that comes from the history of the government's deep suspicion of foreign missionaries. Currently, since virtually all foreign missionaries in China are operating covertly, they often bring with them an element of being a security risk, attracting unwanted attention from the authorities. Even expatriate Asian missionaries are not immune to this challenge.

---

9. Nakah, "Theological Education and the Church in Africa."

One of the major challenges, therefore, is finding a missionary who is linguistically and culturally competent and a local PRC house church that is willing to take the risk of working alongside such a foreign missionary or missionaries. Even though such a partnership is not guaranteed to bear gospel fruit there is tremendous potential for fruitful ministry where partnership exists between the local church and the foreign missionary. Ministry is enhanced when both sides can agree on ministry philosophy, theology and theological vision.[10] In some cases, connecting with a theological heritage or even a common historical creed or confession has great benefits as well.[11]

In the final analysis, we need to realize that the days of pioneering missions in China are a thing of the past except perhaps among certain non-Han ethnic minority groups of China. While imperialism may have bred an unhealthy dependence on foreign support for the Chinese church, nonetheless, the Three-Self model in China has been re-defined to promote a nationalism that isolates the church in the PRC from the global church community. Neither one of these extremes is the answer. Foreign missionaries need to take a more facilitative role, partnering with local churches to produce biblical, sustainable ministry and allowing the PRC church to see a healthy model of connecting with the global church.[12]

Accreditation

One of the greatest needs and biggest challenges to theological education in China is in the area of accreditation. Agencies find it extremely difficult to operate in a context such as the PRC and membership, even as an individual, in large global organizations such as the International Council for Evangelical Theological Educators (ICETE), are often contingent upon being a member of an internationally recognized accrediting association.

Very few PRC house church seminaries have the ability or even the opportunity to seek accreditation through an internationally recognized agency, creating a dead-end for the accrediting process. In 2013 several house church seminaries gathered in Hong Kong to discuss creating an accrediting body that would address this issue from within, rather than from without. What if the PRC house church seminaries created their own national accrediting body? This was the question being asked. This resulted in the founding of an indigenous association of seminaries whose purpose it is to pursue a local accrediting avenue for house church seminaries in the PRC.

10. Keller, *Center Church*.
11. M, "A New Way of Partnership."
12. Steffen, *The Facilitator Era*.

After five years this body has grown from three house church seminaries to twelve, with several others applying to join. For security reasons, it is important to keep the names of these schools and the association anonymous, but as we have slowly made our way forward with this fledgling accrediting body there has been significant interest shown in the accreditation process. There is a need for both indigenous ownership, foreign missionary input and overseas agency guidance as we chart the course ahead. While it is still too early to say what the end results will be, it nonetheless represents an area in the house church where foreign missionaries, with the requisite skills and a humble attitude, can provide meaningful and needed input.

Conclusion

Theological education in the Asian context is young but growing fast and China may very well be the proverbial poster child for this statement. In a very short period, the church has not only experienced an astounding number of converts but in that same short time, it has moved from infancy to adolescence. Possessing all of the weaknesses and abilities of a teenager about to spring into adulthood, the church has moved beyond the more elementary needs of the 1980s and 1990s when foreign missionaries were mostly doing much of the evangelism and discipleship on college campuses throughout China while very few were working directly with the house church.

While there may always be a place for foreign missionaries engaging in these more elementary forms of service to the church in China, the church could easily carry out much of this on their own. Indeed, the church is already doing much of this and many would argue that they are doing it better than the missionaries. What the church is not fully able to do right now is to develop theological education on their own. They are making great strides but the role of the missionary in this area is still very much needed. Foreign missionaries with the requisite skills need to help develop this area of ministry in partnership with the house church in China.

Chapter 9

Helping Chinese House Churches Towards Spiritual Growth and Discipleship

G. WRIGHT DOYLE

When the editor invited me to contribute a chapter to this book, my initial response was, "Sure. I can do that." After all, I have devoted an entire book to this topic.[1] I quickly wrote out an outline, the kind that a good third-year seminary student could put together from authoritative sources. I hoped to fill it in with material gleaned from reading and my own experience and planned to start work in January of 2018.

Then, just as I began to write, things began to fall apart in my life. My daughter became seriously ill with third-stage endometriosis, which caused acute pain and resulted in first one surgery in late April and then another in early August. My wife and I began to travel to our daughter's home, eighty miles away, to care for her and our two-year-old grandson while her husband was at work. Before long, I was worn out, and began to experiences a series of "crashes," leading finally to a complete physical breakdown. Meanwhile, I had done no work on this chapter.

On July 19th, 2018, my doctor, a neurologist, told me that I was suffering from physical exhaustion. She ordered me to rest from all my usual work—immediately, completely, and indefinitely.

---

1. Doyle, *Reaching Chinese Worldwide*.

THE MESSENGERS

The original outline was going to start with the Messengers, both we and those whom we hope to equip to teach others. Now I see this with greater clarity.

"KNOW YOURSELF"

My Board had been talking about the need for me to take a sabbatical leave sometime soon. The last one was in 2001. By the time the sabbatical was supposed to start, I had worked so hard to complete all my projects that I wore myself out. Several other stressors, including the deaths of my mother and two close friends, pushed me over the edge. I contracted walking pneumonia and generally collapsed. My wife and I couldn't go to England as planned, so I just stayed home for the four-month leave.

Rather than writing a couple of academic articles, I spent my time seeing four different counselors.

Why? Because I discovered that behind my physical troubles lay several hidden drains on my emotional energy. Over time, and with skilled probing by my counselors, these came to light: My strength was being sapped by resentment, worry, and guilt.

By God's grace, I dealt with these, one-by-one. At the same time, I engaged in more physical exercise. Over a period of months, my health improved and I returned to my previous ministry.

That wasn't the first time my body had arrested my service as a missionary. My first breakdown came in 1978, after only two years in Taiwan, where we were serving with Overseas Missionary Fellowship (now OMF International). Our two years of full-time language study were about to come to an end, and the field director was prepared to assign me to work at China Evangelical Seminary.

He changed his mind after my doctor—an older missionary with long experience—recommended that I go home for a rest. Another missionary physician, after many hours of interviews, concluded that emotional factors were playing a prominent role in my physical breakdown.

We returned to the United States for two years, during which I received counseling, along with Dori, for our marriage was suffering from the stresses of living overseas and from my own internal struggles. The pastor of our church was recommending Larry Crabb's books at the time, so I dutifully read a couple of them.

I've forgotten how it happened, but something Crabb said pierced my heart. I realized that my motives for going overseas as a missionary were not pure! There was too much self-seeking and pride driving me. After a while, I began to pray for "mixed motives," meaning that I was asking God to put some admixture of good into my otherwise selfish reasons for becoming a missionary.

You would think that I would learn from experiences from these, wouldn't you? Well, I may be the world's slowest learner. I broke down again in 2013, mostly from overwork but also as a result of some sinful patterns in my life. Now, in August, 2018, here I am again, unable to fulfill the ministry I thought God had given me, because my body won't let me. When the doctor told me to take a rest, I asked, "So, what should I do during this time? I don't even know what 'rest' means."

She looked me straight in the eye and said, "Be quiet and let God speak to you."

In the providence of God, over the past year several people have recommended books to me that get to the motives of the heart and how they drive us. Some address the huge problem of addictions of various sorts among Christians; others speak to Christian leaders who are burnt out or who struggle to know God's love in a way that is not simply notional and intellectual. Reading these books has exposed idols and addictions in my own life, causing me to ask God to grant inner transformation and renewal.

One author—Bill Gaultiere—had helped me realize that I am a workaholic. I hadn't seen this before, partly because I don't have some of the usual marks of someone who's addicted to his work. I am strict about resting on Sundays, I take a regular noonday siesta, I have a long quiet time with the Word and prayer every morning, etc. Gaultiere's diagnostic quiz went beyond outward activities to inward drives, however, and revealed to me that my ministry had become an idol to me. I was looking for my writing and personal work to give me significance, a sense of achievement, and security. I had told this to Dr. Roy, who is a neurologist. That is why she told me to "be quiet and let God speak to you."

Now, with time on my hands, I picked the mostly unfinished books up again and began to read with even more attentiveness.

My daughter has found the Enneagram system of describing different personality types helpful, and recommended that I read *The Road Back to You: An Enneagram Journey to Self-Discovery*.[2] Not having finished the book yet, I can't endorse it, but I found several chapters helpful. It seems that, in their language, I am a combination of a "One"—a perfectionist—and a "Two"—a Helper. Each has both positive and negative aspects. In my case, perfectionism makes me very hard on myself and critical (at least mentally)

---

2. Cron and Stabile, *The Road Back to You*.

of people who don't measure up to my standards. And being a "helper" means that I have an inordinate desire for the attention, affection, and approval of others, leading me to try to "help" people even when they don't want it or I don't have the capacity to be of use to them. You can see how these traits could lead to burnout.

THE NEED FOR, AND GOAL OF, SPIRITUAL GROWTH AND DISCIPLESHIP

You may be wondering why I have taken so much time talking about myself. (And I haven't even told you how I lost my voice in Chinese language school under the tutelage of a woman who looked liked my mother, or how I got fired from my position as a seminary faculty member by a president who bore a striking resemblance to my father!)

Isn't this supposed to be a discussion of how to help Chinese house churches grow in spirituality and discipleship?

Discerning readers, especially those who have gone through burnout or breakdowns, will probably be smiling with comprehension, however. They know why I opened this way. By now, they have learned that many, perhaps most, of our attempts to help others toward spiritual maturity and faithful discipleship fall far short of our expectations. They are aware, too, that the main obstacle standing in the way of effective ministry is the minister! As the cartoon character Pogo said long ago, "We have met the enemy and they are us!"

Our own spiritual immaturity and flawed efforts to follow Christ faithfully often render us ineffective in our efforts to nurture spiritual growth in others.

Please do not misunderstand me. I am not saying that you have to go through some sort of collapse to help Chinese house churches to grow. Nor do I believe that any of us can or should come to complete self-knowledge, much less root out all our hidden idols, before we can begin to assist others in spiritual growth and faithful discipleship. We must start where we are and do our best with what we have.

On the other hand, I wish I had listened more carefully to what others, especially my wife Dori, have been trying to tell me for many decades now.

Here's my point: I was dramatically born again in 1965. Since then, I have spent at least twenty minutes reading and meditating on the Bible, and at least that much time in prayer, every day of my life. Usually, it's been more than double or triple that minimum. I've read many books on the Christian life, and have written a few myself. Over the years, I've benefitted from excellent teaching from the pulpit and fine Christian counseling, both for myself and for my marriage. I have a number of prayer partners with whom I share my struggles, and receive frequent counsel from several mature mentors.

And yet, in my early seventies, I am confronted with the sudden revelation that I've been worshiping idols and in bondage to addictions most of my life, causing pain and loss to myself, my family, and those whom I am serving. Yes, God has been gracious, and I treasure his mercy more than ever before in the light of my new self-knowledge.

Now, I assume that other missionaries might share struggles similar to mine, if not exactly the same, and that the Chinese Christians in our life will, perhaps, suffer from even more debilitating weaknesses, since they have probably lacked the abundant resources we enjoy. Furthermore, those who have worked among Chinese for a while know that many pastors and active church members burn out after a few years. Often, the pastors then go abroad "for further study," while others leave for another church or simply drop out altogether.[3] With this new awareness of the depth of my sin and the deceptive power of the world and of Satan, I see much of my previous labors differently.

I wish I had aimed much higher—or perhaps I should say, deeper—in my ministry among Chinese. I would have probed my heart and theirs more carefully, and I would have gone beyond leading Bible studies, teaching classes, and giving advice to my Chinese friends. Instead, I would have tried to encourage them to examine their motives, fears, hidden wounds, idols of the heart, and fundamental assumptions.

In other words, I now see the need for missionaries to ask God to examine their hearts to see whether there is any harmful thing there.[4] We must constantly question our motives. I have seen that much of what I do derives in part from a desire to gain the attention and approval of my father, who seemed to value the athletic prowess of my middle brother more than he did my academic success. It's as if I were saying, "Daddy! Look at me! See what I've done!"

If the truth be told, I am often seeking my own name and fame, rather than God's.

Why do we try to help people? Hopefully, we are responding to God's massive mercy in our lives, his constant protection, and his provision of all our needs. He has loved us, so we want to show that same love to others. In addition, however, I've found that my passion for helping comes also from

---

3. Perhaps we can call this, "burnout with Chinese characteristics."
4. Psalm 139:23.

a longing for a depth of intimacy with others that was lacking in my early childhood. That same deficit of affection has fueled several addictions that I haven't been able to break until recently.

SEEK TO KNOW GOD AND HIS SON JESUS CHRIST

The Bible everywhere warns against idolatry.[5] Both we and our Chinese friends need to learn to love God alone with all our heart, soul, mind, and strength.[6] Instead of vainly trying to build broken cisterns that can't hold water—that is, seeking to find "life," happiness, fulfillment, meaning, etc., in people, pleasure, or our performance as Christian workers—we should be coming constantly to God, the fountain of life.[7] Our wounded, broken, and hungry hearts cry out for love. Jesus says, "I am the bread of life. He who comes to me shall never hunger, and he who believes in Me shall never thirst."[8] We are all dying of thirst; we are thirsty for affection, attention, and approval. Jesus knows that, and says, "If anyone thirsts, let him come to Me and drink."[9]

As we find our satisfaction in Christ, we shall be able to direct our Chinese brothers and sisters to him as the never-failing source of all that they desperately seek. Indeed, only as we ourselves eat and drink of the abundance of God's house[10] will we be able to lead people to the one who gave himself that we might have life—spiritual life, not physical life—in all its abundance.[11]

The need for spiritual growth and discipleship is clear: We and our fellow Chinese believes need to turn from idols and serve the one true and living God.[12] Only then will be mature members of the Body of Christ, and only then will we be able to help others grow into the "measure of the stature of the fullness of Christ."[13]

For that to happen we must know ourselves and we must do all we can to draw upon the immeasurable riches of the love of Christ through faith within the fellowship of other believers.[14]

---

5. See, for Example, Exodus 20:1–3 and 1 John 5:13.
6. Matthew 22:37.
7. Psalm 36:9.
8. John 6:35.
9. John 7:37.
10. Psalm 36:8.
11. John 10:10.
12. 1 Thessalonians 1:9.
13. Ephesians 4:13
14. Ephesians 3:14–21.

In summary: Both missionaries and those whom they serve have deep personal needs that only God can meet, and powerful desires that only he can satisfy. We all need to increase in our ability to draw upon the riches of God's grace in Christ.

THE MEASURE, OR, THE GOAL

The measure of spirituality and discipleship toward which we are aiming is nothing than the likeness of Christ, therefore.[15] We know that he loved God with his entire being. He delighted in the "Law"—that is, the written revelation—of God, and meditated on it day and night.[16] He sought to do only the will of the Father, not his own will.[17] A passion for God's glory, not his own name and fame, drove him, even to the cross.[18]

In all his dealing with people, he sought their good, not his personal "happiness," comfort, safety, or even his life in this world: He came not to be served, but to serve, and to give his life as a ransom for many.[19]

In other words, he was motivated by a pure love of God and for the people he came to save.[20] Paul knew this at the core of his being, and described Jesus as the one "who loved me and gave himself for me."[21]

The goal of all our efforts to grow in grace and to help others develop into mature disciples of Christ, is substantial likeness to Jesus.

THE MESSAGE

With that high standard in mind, we must proclaim—in public and in private—a God-centered, Christ-focused message.

The Gospel

We start with God, as Jesus did. He spoke of "the kingdom of God," a realm where the Supreme Lord of the universe rules.[22] Not shying away from

15. Ephesians 4:13; Philippians 2:5-9; 1 John 3:4.
16. Psalm 1:2.
17. Matthew 26:39, 42; John 4:5; and often in John.
18. John 17:1
19. Mark 10:45.
20. John 11:36; 13:1.
21. Galatians 2:20; see also Ephesians 5:2, 325.
22. Matthew 4:17; and often in the Gospels.

hard truth, he called all people to believe in and submit to the Creator and Governor of all humanity. This universal King, who is completely righteous and utterly holy, demands total allegiance and absolute obedience to all his revealed will.[23] A just and fair sovereign, he richly rewards all who, relying on his grace, attempt to serve him at any cost.[24] On the other hand, Jesus plainly warned that people who stubbornly refuse to do God's will can expect nothing other than everlasting damnation.[25]

This great and majestic God not only brought the world and all mankind into being, but he also chose Abraham and his descendants from among all other peoples to be his special people. Through his prophets, he made known to them his ways and his will in the Holy Scriptures.[26] He instituted a sacrificial system so that sinful people could draw near to him without being consumed by his wrath. He chose David to be the king and founder of an enduring dynasty.

When the Jews rebelled, he chastened them severely, but he did not abandon them. On the contrary, he promised to send to them a Savior, who would deliver them from the guilt and the power of their sins and who would finally establish an eternal kingdom in which righteousness dwells.[27] In due time, he sent his only Son, who is equal with him in every way, to become a man.

This man, Jesus, lived among us, taught God's truth, fully obeyed all God's commands, healed the sick and cast out demons, and demonstrated that he was the promised Savior. When he told the Jewish leaders that they were not righteous, but self-righteous, they persuaded the Roman governor to kill Jesus. To everyone's surprise, Jesus rose from the dead on the third day. After appearing to his disciples for more than a month, he ascended to heaven, where he now sits at the right hand of God the Father.

His death paid the penalty for our sins. Now, he sends his Holy Spirit to free us from the power of indwelling sin and to guarantee that someday he will raise us from the dead with glorified bodies to live with him forever.[28]

All who repent of their sins and fully trust in Christ will be saved from God's wrath.[29] They will receive the Holy Spirit and be born again.[30] Now

---

23. Matthew 5:35; 7:25.
24. Matthew 5:2–12; 6:4, 6.
25. Matthew 5:29–30; 25:30, 36; and many times in the Gospels.
26. Psalm 147:19–20.
27. Matthew 1:21; 2 Peter 3:13.
28. See Romans 8:1–4, 9–17, 19–21, 30.
29. Romans 5:9; 1 Thessalonians 1:10.
30. Acts 2:37–39; 3:19–20; 1 Peter 1:3–4.

they are God's beloved children.[31] They can come to God the Father at any time, asking him to forgive their sins each day and calling upon him to give them the power to follow in the footsteps of Jesus.[32]

But what do we mean by "sin"? In Chinese, the word means "crime," and is often summed up by the phrase, "arson and murder." No, "sin" includes any lack of conformity to the will of God.[33] The Ten Commandments sum up the moral law of God[34] (even if there is some disagreement about the binding nature of the Sabbath command, the principle of taking one day a week as holy began with creation). Jesus and his apostles filled out these commands in a way that God wants us to love him with all our heart, soul, mind, and strength, and to love our neighbor as ourselves.[35]

With Chinese, we must be specific: All idolatry of any kind, outward or internal, is sin. That means that making anything, including our parents, money, "face," food, or success, more important to us than God, is sin. Idolatry is also self-defeating, because it deflects us from the only true source of life and deceives us into seeking happiness outside of God, as my own example testifies. Idols pay poor wages. In fact, they bring death to us. No wonder John ended his first letter with the exhortation, "Little children, keep yourselves from idols."[36]

In today's climate, we must also issue clear warnings against not only individual idols, but corporate ones, such as Chinese culture, traditional Chinese belief systems like Confucianism and Daoism, social influence, and national salvation. Christian history is replete with tragic examples of trying to combine Christianity with another system of thought, lusting after the approval of unbelievers or even influence in society, or seeking to "use" Christianity to achieve national greatness.[37] These temptations assail both Chinese church leaders and their congregations, and stand right in the way of spiritual growth and faithful following of Jesus Christ.

God expects those who believe in Christ to imitate the example of Jesus.[38] They are to reflect his love for the unlovely, his complete faith in God,

---

31. Romans 8:14–17; Colossians 3:12.
32. Matthew 6:12–13. Hebrews 4:14–16.
33. 1 John 3:4.
34. Exodus 20:1–17.
35. Matthew 22:37–40.
36. 1 John 5:20.
37. For the ways in which American Christians have tried to "use" Christianity to save their nation, see G. Wright Doyle, *Christianity in America: Triumph and Tragedy* (Eugene, OR: Wipf & Stock, 2013).
38. See Luke 9:23; John 8:12; Romans 15:2–3; 1 Corinthians 11:1; Ephesians 5:2; 1 Peter 2:21–24; 1 John 3:3; and often.

and his total self-denial, even to the point of death. We must be aware that following Jesus, though it brings many spiritual benefits, and even sometimes some material blessings, always involves daily death to self and to this world. Our hope is not in this world, but in the return of Jesus Christ.

By now, you are probably saying, "But this message is too long! It is too complicated! It will turn people off!"

Let us remember our goal: To help people grow spiritually and in discipleship. How can we expect Christians to become mature followers of Christ if we do not, from the very beginning, tell them the whole truth? Indeed, this message, or some variation of upon it, must form the basis of all our teaching and preaching, both public and private.

Before leaving this all-important topic, I want to emphasize that the Christian gospel is a message of grace. Though God expects us to follow after holiness, he knows we will daily fail to meet his standards of perfection. When we do, we need only humbly admit our sins, ask for his forgiveness, and trust entirely in the blood of Jesus his Son to cleanse us from the guilt and stain of sin.[39] As beloved, though often disobedient, children of God, we may at all times boldly approach the throne of grace to receive mercy and grace to help in time of need.[40]

We don't have to try to hide our offenses from God; he knows about them anyway. Nor do we have to earn his love; he demonstrated his unchanging love for us at the cross.[41] We are justified—considered entirely righteous—entirely by faith in Jesus Christ and, by faith, we stand in the presence of God in a position of total, unconditional acceptance.[42]

That means that all attempts to justify our worth based on performance are both unnecessary and blasphemous, for they deny the finished work of Christ upon the cross for our salvation. If I had believed this more fully, I would not have worn myself out trying to prove my value by writings, and I would not have sought the attention, affection, and approval of other people so much that I ruined my health.

This message, then, is both the fundamental gospel for unbelievers, as well as the daily food for believers. As we teach and preach this liberating truth, we will see people grow into mature and happy followers of Jesus Christ.

At this point, I should say that some people are advocating that we change this basic message to make it more compatible with traditional Chinese culture and thought. I fully believe that we can make use of "points

---

39. 1 John 1:9–2:2.
40. Hebrews 4:16.
41. Romans 5:8.
42. Romans 5:1–2.

of contact" in presenting Christianity to Chinese people.[43] On the other hand, several recent attempts to re-frame the gospel, though written by well-intentioned and learned authors, risk the danger of obscuring the core of the gospel.[44] Beginning with the Apostolic Fathers and down through the centuries, church history is littered with the wreckage of unsuccessful schemes to accommodate biblical truth to pagan philosophy and religion.

The "whole counsel of God"[45]

With this foundation, we can build a structure of comprehensive truth that will help Chinese believers grow into mature spirituality and discipleship. I'll only mention a few basic principles.

First, we should expose them to whole sections of the Bible, not just isolated stories or verses.

In our instruction, we will introduce Chinese believers and seekers to major biblical themes. These include:

God: Traditional Chinese culture and religion have no concept of God, as Jonathan Chao said long ago. That is why I begin my evangelism with God as Creator, Sustainer, Provider, Savior, and Judge. If the greatest command is to love God, then we have to tell our Chinese friends what this God is like, what he has done, and how he wants to relate to us.

In particular, we need to emphasize that Christ's work for us has opened up to us the inestimable privilege of knowing God as our loving, all-powerful heavenly Father.[46] We can tell him all about all we think we need, and trust him to supply all that we really need. When we sin, he will gently receive us back into his warm embrace; all we have to do is repent (again), confess (again), and trust (again).

Christ: Is Jesus just another "god" to add to the pantheon of larger-than-life beings to whom we go for material benefits? Or is he the almighty, eternal Son of God, equal with the Father, who chose to take on human nature, live among us, die for our salvation, and then rise from the dead?[47]

---

43. See Doyle, *Reaching Chinese Worldwide*, 101–140.

44. For reviews of two such recent proposals, see http://www.globalchinacenter.org/analysis/christianity-in-china/theosis-sinochristian-theology-and-the-second-chinese-enlightenment-part-ii.php; and http://www.globalchinacenter.org/analysis/reviews/weaknesses-in-general-wu-makes.php.

45. Acts 20:27.

46. See, for example, Matthew 6:9–15, 25–34; 7:7–12; Romans 8:14–17.

47. Matthew's Gospel contains a comprehensive portrait of Christ. G. Wright Doyle, *Christ the King: Meditations on Matthew's Gospel* (Durham, NC: Light Messages, 2011) is a devotional commentary on Matthew that focuses on Christ as God, Man, and King.

Christians must know that our Christ rules the universe with his powerful word, that he prays for us with understanding and compassion, and that he will come again in glory for his people.[48]

The Holy Spirit: Is the Holy Spirit an impersonal force? No, he is the Third Person of an eternal Trinity; he is the Spirit of the Father and of the Son, whom God gives to those who truly repent and trust in Christ.[49] He comes into our hearts with life-transforming power in the work of regeneration, which is his doing, not ours.[50] Chinese Christians use a phrase that means, "regeneration and salvation," to refer to a human action that consists of simply praying to receive Christ. But these words really refer to God's sovereign work in the soul, not to our action, and the regenerating power and presence of the Spirit manifest themselves in a radically changed life.[51]

To grow in spirituality and in discipleship, we need to call upon the divine work of the Holy Spirit, received daily by faith, to effect miracles of moral liberation and renewal in those constantly repent and trust in him.[52] Simply teaching believers about the disciplines of the Christian life (the "means of grace") will not produce mature Christians. They need to learn how to call upon God the Spirit to take the Scriptures and use them for the renewal of their minds.[53]

Spiritual growth also requires knowledge of biblical teaching on Christian living, such as is found in the Sermon on the Mount (Matthew 5–7), instructions on faithful and costly witness (Matthew 10), and the ethical portions of the epistles.[54] These tell us how to live in the family, the church, and society.

The Old Testament: Too many Chinese Christians, like their brothers and sisters in the rest of the world, do not know even the outlines of God's dealing with his people as told in the Old Testament.[55] We must find ways to fill this gap. The Psalms will teach them how to worship and pray,

---

48. Hebrews 1:3; 4:14–15; 7:25; Romans 8:34; Acts 1:11.
49. Acts 2:33, 38.
50. John 3:3–5.
51. See, for example Galatians 5:22–23.
52. See Galatians 3:3–5.
53. Psalm 119:9, 11; Ephesians 4: 23.
54. For example, Romans 6, 8, 12–14; 1 Corinthians 5–14; Galatians 5:22–6:10; Ephesians 4:1–6:20; Philippians 2:1–11; 4:4–9; Colossians 3:1–4:6; Titus; Hebrews 12–13; James; 1 Peter; etc.;
55. For examples from the apostles, see Romans 4:1–25; 5:12–21; 9:6–29; 1 Corinthians 10:1–13; Hebrews 11.

especially in times of trouble, and Proverbs will give practical guidance for daily living.[56]

Marriage and family: Christian marriages form the core of the church. Most Chinese, including Christians, have very little concept of what marriage according to God's plan looks like. Detailed, specific, teaching on this vital subject will help believers to grow spiritually and in mature discipleship. Likewise, we should explain what the Bible teaches about bringing up children "in the training and admonition [instruction] of the Lord,"[57] so that the next generation of believers can face the temptation so the world, enjoy God's blessings, and reflect his glory in society.[58]

The necessity of suffering: In my experience, stunted spiritual growth and faltering discipleship have resulted not just from the temptations of the world but also from encountering difficulty. Chinese, especially, must know that our God never promised us that if we believe in him and follow Jesus, things will go easily for us. Jesus solemnly said, "In the world you will have trouble."[59]

We must warn people to expect trouble of all sorts in following Christ, from the world, the flesh, and the devil. Scriptures about facing trials will help our friends weather the inevitable storms of the Christian life.[60]

Life in the church: We do not advance in our spiritual life or in discipleship alone. All believers are part of the Body of Christ, each with a spiritual gift to use in serving others in love. Our people will grow as they understand and apply the biblical passages on life in the church.[61] Since nothing blocks spiritual growth more than conflict with other Christians that is not resolved biblically, we must offer specific teaching on how to resolve differences and disputes.[62]

---

56. See G. Wright Doyle, *Worship and Wisdom* (Durham, NC: TorchFlame Books, 201).

57. Ephesians 64

58. See G. Wright Doyle, *The Good, the Bad, and the Beautiful: A Handbook to Marriage*, Durham, NC: TorchFlame Books, 2018, for some basic teaching.

59. John 16:33.

60. The Psalms are full of prayers to use in time of trouble of all sorts. For other relevant passages on suffering, see also the Gospels; much of the Book of Acts; Romans 8:18–39; 2 Corinthians 1:3–11; 4:7–18; 12:7–10; 2 Timothy 2:1–13; 3:10–12; Hebrews 11; James 1:2–18; 5:10–13; 1 Peter 1:3–10; 4:1–2, 12–19; 5:6–11; and the Book of Revelation.

61. See, for example, Romans 12:1–21; 1 Corinthians 12–14; Ephesians 4:1–32; 1 Peter 4:7–11.

62. See Matthew 7:1–12 (and see my article, "Pearls, Pigs, and the Golden Rule," at https://www.academia.edu/27018453/PEARLS_PIGS_AND_THE_GOLDEN_RULE_A_Fresh_Look_at_Matthew_7_1-12); Matthew 18:15–20; Ephesians 4:15–26.

Our future hope: Chinese describe themselves as "pragmatic," and they are right! For millennia, Chinese have focused on life in this world, not on hope for a world to come. Some Buddhists, of course, defy this characterization, but most Chinese who call themselves "Buddhists" go to the temple to ask for material and worldly benefits, not for eternal life. To counter this powerful obsession—for it is an obsession—we must constantly remind our friends that our hope is in heaven, not on earth. As Peter urged, we are to "set our hope fully on the grace to be revealed to us when Christ appears."[63] Christ and the apostles regularly and insistently taught people to look not for health and worldly happiness in this life, but to place our expectations for satisfaction, safety, security, and every other ultimate desire upon the world to come when Christ returns.[64]

Meditation upon Scripture and Memorization of the Bible: We grow into mature disciples of Christ by feeding on the Word of God.[65] Individually and corporately, followers of Christ can make no spiritual progress unless they "let the word of Christ dwell in [them] richly." Teaching and showing how to saturate our minds with the Word of God are by far the most important thing we can do to help Chinese believers mature as his disciples.

In conclusion, I shall only briefly mention several other important elements of disciple-making:

MEETINGS

For too long, we have directed our energies toward producing large gatherings of believers in a building dedicated to religious activity. Recent government policy threatens to make this method of spiritual growth more and more difficult, if not impossible. As I have argued elsewhere, however, the New Testament strongly implies that home meetings are the norm for Christian gatherings.[66] From the time that Constantine made it possible for large numbers of people to gather in big buildings, through the Middle Ages, to the present, history shows that the bigger the congregation, the more likely we are to see stunted spiritual growth and lukewarm discipleship.

Instead, we should nurture smaller fellowships meeting in homes, where real Christian fellowship can take place. Evangelism that produces

---

63. 1 Peter 1:13.

64. A small sample would include Matthew 5:3–12; Luke 10:20; Romans 8:18–30; 1 Corinthians 1:7–9; 15:19, and all of that chapter; 2 Corinthians 4:7–18; 2 Peter 3:10–13; 1 John 3:1–3; the Book of Revelation.

65. 1 Peter 2:1–3.

66. Doyle, " A Theology for House Churches."

true followers of Christ takes place best in intimate gatherings; the same is true for Christian instruction, corporate prayer, participatory worship, modeling the Christian life, and gentle correction.

Nor should we neglect one-to-one meetings or discipleship done with only two or three people.

MEN

Yes, men; as in males. The preponderance of women in Chinese house churches presents one of the most serious challenges to healthy spiritual growth. Millions of Christian women seek in vain for a fellow believer to marry.[67] The church needs Christian fathers to reflect the fatherhood of God, and mature men to serve as elders.[68] Jesus did not neglect women—far from it!—but he devoted most of his time to "the training of the Twelve." Male missionaries must do the same.[69]

METHODS

Finally, a few words about methods.[70]

Given the fundamental principles I have outlined above, several things will seem obvious:

First, we must go slow, go small, and go deep. If we are to help people grow to full spiritual maturity and faithful discipleship, we must avoid the temptation to produce quick results, gather big crowds, and seek "success" in numbers of converts. Not only do current conditions in China demand such an approach, but the example of Jesus and of Paul point us toward a quest for quality, not quantity. Both men preached to large audiences, but both made it clear that lasting conversions result from the sovereign work of God and that true discipleship manifests itself in changed lives, not mere

---

67. For a discussion of the nature, possible causes, and potential solutions to this crisis, see http://www.globalchinacenter.org/analysis/christianity-in-china/gender-imbalance-in-the-chinese-church-causes-consequences-and-possible-cures.php.

68. This is a very controversial subject, I know, but no one can deny the need for men to serve as leaders in the church. See

69. I have attempted to address this need in G. Wright Doyle, *Jesus: the Complete Man*, Bloomington, IN: AuthorHouse, 2008. The [traditional character] Chinese edition is titled, *Confucius and Jesus*). Also "A Real Man," https://chinainstitute.squarespace.com/a-real-man.

70. For much more on the wide variety of methods we can employ, see Doyle, *Reaching Chinese Worldwide*, 71–100, 157–178.

verbal professions of faith.[71] We must aim for nothing less than the renovation of the mind that produces a transformed life.[72]

Prayer: Following Jesus,[73] Paul sets the example here. His prayers reflect the theological convictions that make sense of my experience, namely, that we are all profoundly "broken" in our inner mind, prone to worship idols, in bondage to misdirected loves and drives, and desperately needing the intervention of God on a daily basis. Our prayers for those under our care should resemble his, as we ask God to show his wisdom, power, and love;[74] fill his people with love, discernment, and the "fruits of righteousness that are by Jesus Christ";[75] transform their lives, strengthen them by his power, filling their hearts with gratitude;[76] and "direct [their] hearts into the love of God and into the patience of Christ."[77]

Power? Some say that "signs and wonders" must accompany our life and message. Others deny the relevance of New Testament experiences to our own day. I believe that we can and should pray for God to work miracles of healing and exorcism, and teach our converts to do the same. At the same time, we need to remind them that God is sovereign, and may withhold healing for his own purposes. We can, to be sure, cast out demons in the name of Jesus.[78] And we should seek the health of those who follow Christ, but we cannot lead them to believe that God will fully heal every illness in this life.[79] More importantly, we can ask God to work the greater miracle of a changed life in those who follow Christ.[80]

Problematic practices: As I explain more fully in *Reaching Chinese Worldwide*, several common practices lack sufficient biblical support to continue using them.[81] Perhaps the most egregious of these is the widespread—almost universal—habit of asking people to "pray to receive Christ,"

---

71. See Matthew 4:25; 7:21–27; 8:18–22; 13:1–9, 18–23; John 3:3–5; 6:37, 44–46, 65; Galatians 5:22–23; Ephesians 1:15; 5:1–7; Philippians 3:17–20; 1 Thessalonians 1:9–10; 2:13–14; 2 Thessalonians 1:3–5; and often.

72. See Romans 12:1–2; Ephesians 4:17–24.

73. John 17.

74. See Ephesians 1:15–23; 3:14–21.

75. Philippians 1:9–11; Colossians 1:9.

76. Colossians 1:9–12.

77. 2 Thessalonians 3:5.

78. Mark 16:17–18.

79. See G. Wright Doyle, *The Lord's Healing Words* (Bloomington, IN: AuthorHouse, 2006).

80. For more on this and other problematic practices, see Doyle, *Reaching Chinese Worldwide*, 85–95.

81.

and then to count those who "PRC" as Christians. First, the apostles neither taught nor followed such a practice. Instead, they called to repent, believe, and be baptized. As I said above, they considered faithful involvement in a local Christian gathering and changed conduct to be signs that a person had become a follower of Christ.

Presence: Just as Jesus dwelt among his people, manifesting his grace and truth to them, and Paul lived out his teaching before his converts, including Timothy, so we should let our Chinese friends see us up close and in action, at home, in the church, and in the world.[82] By his own example, Jesus taught the disciples how to live and how to share the gospel in a convincing way, even unto death.[83] We must do the same.[84]

CONCLUSION

So, we are now back where we started, with the Messengers. As messengers of the gospel of Jesus Christ, we need to ask our risen Lord to reproduce his character in us, that we may show the way as well as teach it, daily admitting to them our wickedness (though perhaps not in all its detail), our weakness, our woundedness, and our resistance to Satan's devices.[85] Relying entirely on the strength of the Risen Lord, and gazing in faith upon his glory as revealed in Scripture,[86] we shall provide a pattern of true spiritual growth and faithful discipleship, so that we can say, "Imitate me, just as I also imitate Christ."[87]

---

82. John 1:14; 1 Thessalonians 2:1–12 2 Timothy 3:10–12

83. Philippians 2:5–11; 1 Peter 2:21–25.

84. For more on the importance of presence, see Doyle, *Reaching Chinese Worldwide*, 59–60, 66–67.

85. As Paul did. See Romans 7:13–25; 2 Corinthians 1:8–11; 4:7–14; 6:4–10; 12:7–10.

86. 2 Corinthians 3:18.

87. 1 Corinthians 11:1.

PART IV

Other Key Components in China's Harvest Fields

Chapter 10

A Humble and Sacrificial Mission

CHEN JING

One of the most critical developments within the house church movement in China in recent years has been its new vision and energy for global missions.[1] If overseas, cross-cultural missions from Chinese house churches was just a little stream in the past, it is now on its way to becoming a mighty river. Never before has the Chinese Church embraced the vision of their all-out participation in missions in such an enthusiastic and organized way. As a result, such an internationally known platform as Mission China 2030 has been launched, mission agencies and training schools are mushrooming, and an increasing number of missionaries are being sent from the country. Needless to say, these rising mission initiatives are pumping in much-needed new blood to the global mission movement, and generating new excitement and appreciation from the Christian family around the world.

CHALLENGES AND ISSUES

As Chinese Church observers, supporters, and partners, we of course thank God for our Chinese brothers and sisters' passion for mission, and cheer them on, and forge new partnerships in world mission. However, if we truly

---

1 For an overview of the cross-cultural movement of the Chinese Protestant Church, please see the article: "The Chinese Church: The Next 'Superpower' in World Mission?" *Evangelical Missions Quarterly*, July 2014, Vol.50, No.3, 296–303.

love Chinese believers, we should become concerned, when we see the external and internal challenges facing them. Let me just name a few of them.

A. Externally, the Chinese authorities are watching the Chinese Church's push for global missions very closely and nervously. And it is difficult to predict how they are going to react to it. But their initial response sounds ominous. For example, in the wake of the martyrdom of two young Chinese missionaries in Pakistan in 2017, their sending church network in Wenzhou was under the governmental pressure. In addition, mission fields the Chinese Church is focusing on are largely Islamic countries and regions. And backlash, persecution, and even martyrdom is anticipated there.

B. The massive global mission movement envisioned by the Chinese Church is unprecedented in the Chinese church history. Not surprisingly, the Chinese Church has very little experience in setting up necessary organizational structures, recruiting, supporting, and training missionaries. And the lack of adequate cross-cultural training and preparation for Chinese missionaries is already well known among the international missionary community.

C. So far, the Chinese Christian communities'—including overseas Chinese churches'—approach to global missions remains overwhelmingly managerial and technical. And any meaningful, deep reflection on mission theology and history is still missing. As a result, there are signs of missiological disorientation and confusion, and highly questionable theological arguments are put forward for global missions for the Chinese Church. For example, national prosperity and strength are identified and exaggerated as the driving force behind global missions in modern times. Therefore, China's rise as a political and economic superpower and the expansion of the country's influence through the so-called "one-road, one belt" scheme are considered signs from God and a powerful motivation for the Chinese Church to join global missions. The resulting rhetoric, such as "it's Chinese Christians' turn to carry the baton of the gospel back to Jerusalem" are getting popular and not being challenged at all among Chinese believers. However, talks like that smack of nationalism and triumphalism, and may mislead the Chinese Church to future disaster in the mission fields.

Out of all these three factors, in my opinion, the first one is beyond our control, and the second one is very much technical in nature. And the third one would perhaps have the most profound and lasting impact on the Chinese mission movement. If we do not have a biblically sound missiological starting point and foundation for missions, then we are not clear about what kind of missions the Chinese Church would bring to the rest of the world, and subsequently the Chinese Church's global impact would be likely negative. That is why I will focus on missiological orientation of the Chinese Church's global missions in this chapter. I intend to illustrate a biblically based mission with humility and servanthood, and draw positive and negative lessons from mission history, and encourage Chinese believers to imitate Jesus Christ in their mission endeavors. Finally, I will offer some suggestions about how we can partner with the Chinese Church in advancing the gospel in Jesus' way.

THE HUMILITY OF JESUS

According to John 20-21, "again Jesus said, peace be with you! As the Father has sent me, I am sending you." Indeed, God send us into the world, just as He sent Jesus. Therefore, Jesus Christ is our example or role model in missions. What does Jesus's mission look like? First of all, Jesus' mission is from the Father, and of total obedience to Him. Second, his mission is one of total humility, self-giving, self-sacrifice, and complete surrender. Thirdly, His mission does not depend on human might, power, resources, skills, or schemes. Instead, he shows us what is total dependence on God's leading and power.

In Philippians 2:5-8, Paul sums up Jesus' ministry this way: "Your attitude should be the same as that of Christ Jesus: Who, being in very nature God, did not consider equality with God something to be grasped, but made himself nothing, taking the very nature of a servant, being made in human likeness. And being found in appearance as a man, he humbled himself and became obedient to death—even death on a cross!" In his life and death, Jesus demonstrated to us what is a true mission with humility and servanthood. As Paul said at the beginning of this passage, this is the example Jesus set for us, and this is the kind of attitude we need to emulate from Jesus and take on in missions. There are so many mission models and strategies we can employ in the 21st Century. But none of them can take the place of Jesus's example, and none of them should replace the essential spirit of Jesus' mission. If our missions today loses this essential spirit and nature of Jesus' mission, then our missions will not please God, but instead bring dishonor to God's name.

THE TRIUMPHALISTIC MISSION VS. HUMBLE MISSION IN HISTORY

Too many times over the past two thousand years, the Church in the world failed to resist the temptations of power, status and wealth, and drifted away from the biblical vision of mission. The dire consequences are the Constantinian Settlement, Catholic dominance in medieval Europe, and collaboration between Western colonialism and missionary enterprises. Once churches began to forget the virtues of humility, mercy, and servanthood as the core ethos of Christian missions, they would inevitably take on the Christendom mentality and identify the church and missions with the so-called "Christian nations" or "Christian civilizations." And missionaries were sent out not just as ambassadors of the churches but also as representatives of "superior civilizations or cultures." And they often went out hand-in-hand with imperial armies or colonialists. And missions was carried out in collaboration with the secular political authorities and military might. When a land was conquered and colonized, churches were erected there. Rather than with a humble attitude and behavior, missionaries often arrived on the field with a strong sense of arrogance and superiority, and their relations with natives were often paternalistic and condescending. While These kinds of imperialistic or Christendom mission enterprises contributed to the spread of Christianity, they have definitely led to immensely negative consequences, having smeared the name of the Lord, and tarnished the image of the Church. In the long run, it created huge obstacles for the spreading of the gospel around the world. In China and other parts of the world today, aren't we still dealing with the negative legacy of this kind of unbiblical mission approach? Mission history has over and over again attested to how once the Church intentionally or unintentionally enters into a sort of collaboration with political governments, and begins to depend on the states' protection, taking on ethnic and cultural superiority, the result is disastrous for Christian missions.

In fact, mission history shows us that it has been humble and sacrificial missions not relying on worldly authority and power that have truly glorified the Lord's name, won peoples' hearts, and laid a solid foundation for indigenous churches. Historical models of this kind of missions are not hard to come by: the early church's missions in the Book of Acts; the monastic movement and Nestorian missions in medieval times; and, the China Inland Mission (CIM) in modern times.

From the first to the third centuries the Church was powerless and without privilege in the world, and often persecuted and marginalized, but totally depended on the power of the Holy Spirit, and spread the good news across the empire. Their secret: completely following and imitating Christ. In modern China, many Western missionaries came with a sense of cultural superiority, as they were depending on the military and political might of Western powers. These missionaries belonged under the protection of the so-called unequal treaties between China and the West. By so doing, these missionaries were relatively safe and secure on the mission field, but they contributed less to the Kingdom of God in China than did the humble missionaries of the CIM. What made the CIM missionaries so special was their willingness to lay down their privilege and identity for the sake of the gospel. By following Christ, they risked everything, went into remote villages and mingled with the lowest of the society, and—in humility becoming Chinese to win the Chinese—adopted average Chinese peoples' lifestyle and language,. When persecution came, they laid down their own life and their families' lives, and willingly paid heavy personal prices, rather than appealing to clauses in treaties and demanding the punishment of Chinese authorities in the name of "justice." During the infamous "Boxer' Rebellion (1900)," the CIM suffered the most horrible and heaviest loss of property and life among all mission agencies in China, but they refused to claim their "rights" for the sake of Christ. With their own blood and sacrifice, Hudson Taylor and the CIM demonstrate to us what a humble, sacrificial and Christ-like mission means. With their tremendous achievements in evangelism and church -planting, the CIM also testified to a biblical truth: missions depending foremost on God's power, rather than on human power and resources, seem to be weak and feeble, but rather are pleasing to God and used by Him. And their achievements can stand the test of time.

In sharp contrast, those missionaries who benefited from the political and military might of Western powers in China might have helped the mission work and church-planting in China to some extent. But these Western missionaries' historical ties with Western colonialism have become a burden on the shoulders of Christian communities in China, and this burden still exists within the Chinese church today. It often causes problems for missions when Christian missions go hand-in-hand with worldly power and resources. This has been a historical reality all around the world, when missionaries sent are sent worldwide from powerful and rich countries.

It is undeniable that the industrialization of Western countries provided modern missions with the necessary infrastructure such as financial resources and technological means (transportation and communication). We have good reason to thank God for these modern conveniences. However, it would be an exaggeration if we considered the infrastructure as the necessary conditions and primary driving forces behind global missions in modern times. In fact, the major driving force should be hundreds and thousands of believers' commitment and sacrifice under the guidance of the Holy Spirit. Without this, Christian missions is impossible.

CHINESE MISSIONS AND THE RISE OF CHINA

Lessons from mission history are especially relevant to Chinese missions today, because the Chinese Church today is often compared with European and American churches of the 19th Century. And the argument is made that the churches developed in world missions, when their respective countries rose in economic power and international influence. As was explained above, the correlation between missions and national power has existed in history. This correlation has become missiologically misleading and detrimental, particularly when we have not put this correlation in a proper perspective, and have treated it as the major driving force and justification for missions. It would be very harmful, because it can easily lead to a truimphalistic mission approach.

In my view, this is one of the major temptations the Chinese Church is facing, when it envisions its role in global missions. When Chinese mission mobilizers and oversea supporters of the Chinese mission lay out the case for the Chinese Church's growing role in global missions, not a small number of them would single out the growing economic power and international political clout of China as the larger backdrop, and the increasing resources of the Chinese Church as a direct result. And China's dramatically extending presence and influence in Central Asia, Middle East, South Asia, and Africa through its ambitious "One Road, One Belt" (OROB) scheme is often hailed as a God-given opportunity for Chinese missionaries to go into these strategic regions. In other words, the Chinese Church and its missionaries should fully take advantage of this historical opportunity to join Chinese government-sponsored projects as tent-makers and spread the gospel along the way.

I would not say all these arguments are totally wrong. But in my judgment, all this talk and rhetoric sounds a bit too rosy, naive, and overly optimistic about the OROB and its implications for Christian missions. And it is urgent and necessary for us to realize that the rise of China and the OROB could be a blessing or curse, an opportunity or a pitfall for Chinese missions. If we tie together the OROB and missions unconditionally, we risk fatal dangers. Against this tendency, I would like to give two cautions.

First, the rise of China and the OROB cannot and should not be the fundamental motivation and driving force for the missions from the Chinese Church. Instead, the only biblically legitimate and ultimate missionary motivation is the call of the "Great Commission" from God and His love. This is true for any genuine missions from the past two thousand years, and is also true for Chinese missions today. If that is true, then true biblical missions is the humble and sacrificial mission embodied so powerfully in Jesus' life and death. Besides that, there are absolutely no other alternatives. Yes, China's economic growth has made the Chinese Church resourceful, and large projects like the OROB have opened up a lot of doors for the Church so that Chinese missionaries can go, settle and minister among different people groups in foreign lands. However, if the primary motivation, direction and strategy of missions for the Chinese Church are shaped and decided mainly by the rise of the country and the OROB, this would inevitably be a huge tragedy of the Chinese Church. After all, it is always dangerous to blindly associate the launching of a missionary movement with the rise of a particular nation and its political and economic might.

Secondly, when we talk about following the routes of China's international trade and high-speed train systems in our mission sending, are we unintentionally tying God's missions with the expansion of China's influence? Are we going to bring to the mission field a condescending and arrogant mentality and attitude of the citizens of a global superpower, and thus weaken and lose our ability to live out incarnational and sacrificial love? Are we going to become allies of China's political and economic power in the eyes of the natives one day? When we talk about our grand vision for a global mission from the Chinese Church, do we forget to give all glory to God?

Frankly, all these scenarios are reminiscent of historical mistakes committed by Western missionaries in the 19th Century. Whenever we have such great confidence in our own resources, solutions and protection, and treat them as the pre-conditions absolutely necessary for a successful mission, we may feel safe and powerful for the time being. But the matter of fact is that a mission like that is weakest in God's eyes. Let us never forget "not by might nor by power, but by my spirit," (Zechariah, 4:6) a Christian mission is possible and effective.

LET US WORK TOGETHER WITH THE CHINESE CHURCH IN FOSTERING A HUMBLE SPIRIT

There is no question that the Chinese Church's global mission needs to be grounded in the biblical perspective and teachings, and be modeled on Jesus' obedience, humility and servanthood. And Chinese mission leaders and missionaries need to constantly ask themselves these basic questions: Why do we go out to the mission fields? What kind of mentality should we bring with us? What kind of mission movement are we going to introduce into the world?

Today, as we face unprecedented historical opportunities of global missions, when we are tempted by huge possibilities made possible by the OROB, let us be reminded of how: Jesus Christ came to this world with nothing except God's grace and power, but he turned the world upside down; the CIM under the leadership of J. Hudson Taylor surrendered its privilege and safety in China for the sake of the gospel; and, those young Chinese mission pioneers in the 1940s placed their promising future on the altar, and chose to walk a path of evangelizing and suffering in northwestern China. A mission of humility and sacrifice has been done before, and can be done today. In their suffering and humility, these mission pioneers showed us how whether we have resources or not, whether we are in difficult situations or not, our commitment to God's calling and mandate should remain firm, and our willingness to lay down everything and sacrifice our most precious things for Christ should never change. And no matter what mission fields and contexts we find ourselves in, our core identity should always be the same: we are the ambassadors of the gospel, and all other identities we own on the earth are all secondary.

As more and more Chinese missionaries arrive on the mission field, they will face many temptations and wrestle with many questions. Can we always consider ourselves as servants of God and ambassadors of the gospel, or take pride in our own citizenships of a powerful nation and sophisticated culture? Under any circumstances, can we always take refuge under the fortress provided by God, or constantly wish to be protected by our own government and its power? Can we keep a healthy distance from the political and economic power in the world, while also taking the evangelistic opportunities created by the rise of China? Can we walk out of our own comfort zones, and blend into the native societies, love local people, and adopt their language, lifestyle and culture? Can we let go of any intent to control and dominate, but rather treat local mission workers as equal partners? When persecution comes, and our appealing to governmental protection would hurt the cause of the gospel among the local people, can we yield our own rights, and place ourselves completely in the hand of God? These are hard questions. But if Chinese missionaries' answers to them are "yes," then their mission will definitely be a humble and incarnational mission modeled after Jesus' way.

So far I have laid out the emerging Chinese mission movement's main issues and needs for a sound missiological identity and orientation. As I indicated earlier in this chapter, this movement has numerous needs. But in my opinion, none of them are more important and crucial than this very basic issue of identity and orientation. If we fail to put this movement on the right foundation and right direction, then it will certainly shipwreck down the road. As we from North America contemplate how to partner with the Chinese Church in world missions, we need to start with these basic questions, too. Precisely because they are simple and basic, they are easy to be neglected. Looking back at the mission history of Western churches, we did not always get these questions right. There is no doubt that the global mission movement will witness the waves of resourceful mission endeavors from China, But the Chinese Church's lack of experience may make them vulnerable to triumphalism. We in the West have plenty of positive and negatives lessons we can offer to our Chinese brothers and sisters so that they won't repeat our mistakes. Let us walk with them in doing missions in His way and fulfilling His Great Commission.

Chapter 11

Missionaries Helping Local Churches Reach Unreached People Groups

BARNABAS ROLAND

As foreign missionaries among Chinese UPGs, one of the most important assets that we hold that can help the Chinese church reach Unreached People Groups is our vantage point. We understand and live among the minority groups. We have passion and experience with minority peoples. We have learned from our mistakes on the field as well, and we are able to see the troubles and successes of the American church from an outsider's perspective. We have experienced the painful perseverance of crossing cultures.

Yet, I contend that our vantage point can be limiting. A laser focus on our task of reaching a particular UPG can itself end up becoming a laser focus only on that people group. What is the difference? If we focus exclusively on the people group, we lose sight of the larger task. We are not here just to see one people group reached for Christ. We desire to see that people group also reach other people groups. The task is to see China reach the UPGs of China and the world so that Christ is revealed as glorious Redeemer and ultimate King.

We must evaluate whether or not our own vantage point is limiting us. We know that we are limited if our "racial profiling" keeps us from sharing the gospel with people outside our focus group. Or if we begin to take in a defensive attitude toward the Han Chinese majority. Or if our grand vision is mono-lingual or monoethnic. Or if only one people group is part of our church planting strategy.

In the words of the apostle Paul, Peter was clearly seen as an apostle to the Jews and Paul was called to a ministry to the Gentiles (Gal 2:7–10), but the intention was not to be an exclusive approach. Peter had significant ministry events among the Gentiles, such as with Cornelius the Roman centurion (Acts 10–11). Peter literally needed a vision from God to urge him to share the gospel with this Gentile. When Cornelius and his whole household came to faith, Peter became an instrumental spokesman for widening the scope of the Jerusalem church to see the Gentiles.

Paul, the apostle to the Gentiles, had a tremendous ministry to the Jews. In fact, when there was a Jewish synagogue in a city of his missionary journeys, his pattern was to first to go to the Jewish synagogue. Neither Peter nor Paul had exclusive approaches of just one people group. Moreover, Paul rejected the approach of one culture engulfing another so that Gentiles had to become Jews (Gal 2:7–14). The rejection of this approach is not just for the soteriological reasons having to do with the Jewish law. The Biblical vision is that all families of the earth can be blessed (Gen 12:3) and one day every tongue and tribe will be worshipping God around the throne together (Rev 7:9–10).

Both Peter and Paul struggled greatly with cultural barriers, yet it was often another people group they were not concentrating on that ended up being instrumental in reaching the people groups to whom they were called.

The situation in China today is still similar to Peter and Paul. China is not a monolith. In China, reaching a city does not automatically lead to the people groups of the region around the city being reached. The multicultural globalization of megacities and mono-cultural Sinicizing of China's minority groups have not yet reached such an influence to extinguish the barriers among people groups. The cultural and linguistic divide is obvious today just by reading the news the last few years of the social unrest of the Uyghurs and Tibetans. It still takes intentionality and great effort to overcome the barriers of language and culture so that the mountains of the Southwest are saturated with the gospel.

In order to most effectively reach the unreached people group to whom we are called, we should have multiple people groups in our scope: Unreached People Groups (UPGs), Unengaged, Unreached People Groups (UUPGs), and Reached People Groups (RPGs). On one side if we only focus on reaching one UPG, we limit the workers by failing to mobilize and equip reached people groups. And on the other side once that people group is reached, it becomes more difficult to cast the vision to other people groups if our prayer and vision has only been monoethnic.

In this chapter I will focus on crucial actions to meet the current pressing needs of how foreign workers can reach China's UPGs and UUPGs. But the critical turning point that we often stumble in is how to properly equip missionaries of the churches of Reached People Groups. These RPGs are not merely the Han of the eastern China. There are Han house churches in most of the counties inhabited by the Zhuang of Guangxi, the Li of Hainan, and the Yi of Yunnan. Moreover, missionaries too often forget about the RPGs that live only a county or two away from their people groups. Certain people segments of the Lisu, the Nasu Yi, the Miao, the Yao and several other groups already have majority populations that are Christian. There are many things we can do to mobilize and serve RPGs so that they have their own indigenous catalytic structures for crossing cultures.

The church of China can reach China. We can ask the question of whether or not the church of China is ready. But even more personally we must closely examine whether or not we are ready to equip the church of China. Are we even willing to equip the church of China? This is not a question to breeze by quickly. A limiting vantage point can exacerbate our frustration of equipping national cross-cultural workers simply by limiting our perception for the need to equip them.

ESTABLISH HEALTHY, REPRODUCING CHURCHES AMONG UNREACHED PEOPLE GROUPS (UPGS).

Unreached People Groups (UPGs) are the ethnolinguistic people groups who do not have an indigenous Christian community with enough disciples and appropriate resources to evangelize their own people. The state of the church among a UPG should be the primary determining factor of our missions strategy among that group. The top three pressing church planting needs among Unreached People Groups are evangelism, leadership training, and heart language access to Scripture. Where these elements are flourishing among the UGPs in China, there is usually a correlation of healthy discipleship that is leading to churches being planted and growing to maturity.

When there are few believers and churches, the primary task is evangelism. An expanded understanding of evangelism among UPGs is evangelism that leads to churches as workers enter an area, share the gospel, disciple new believers, gather them together as churches and train indigenous leaders so that these churches plant other healthy, multiplying churches. At this point I will focus on the more narrow understanding of the evangelistic task of sharing the gospel.

We need much more evangelism because there are indeed many people that have not heard of the gospel. Among those that have heard about Christianity, there are many who can only equate Christianity with Hollywood of the "Christian" West. Further complicating the matter is the continued prevalence of quasi-Christian cults. Eastern Lightning and forms of Er Liang Liang such as the Disciples Cult (Mentuhui), that are called Christian (Jidu jiao) in Mandarin, but the hero of their religion is some version of a second Christ figure. The absence of Mandarin literacy, a void of gospel truth, and the prominence of the authority of the teacher have all lent many minority people vulnerable to a message that is almost the gospel. Government persecution of these quasi-Christian cults have caused people to go further underground in their beliefs or reject what they know of Christianity, essentially inoculating them against Christianity.

It will take more than foreign missionaries and local Christian leaders sharing the gospel in their communities. All Christians can be trained to effectively share the gospel. Even new believers can share what they know of the gospel like the woman in the well who shared the excitement of what she knew about Christ: "Many Samaritans from that town believed in him because of the woman's testimony, 'He told me all that I ever did.'" (John 4:39).

Workers can shape their ministry strategies so that they can receive short-term workers (a few weeks or months), mid-term workers (a few months to a few years), and long-term workers so that more Christian witnesses are living among the people group. Long-term workers often need someone to create pathways for them to work and live there, but even short-term and mid-term workers can add extremely effectively to the witness. But all the workers need to be trained well so that they just don't attend a session to hand out gospel tracts. They need opportunities for long-term workers to model how to share the gospel, and help from us working alongside them and coaching them.

If evangelism is the primary need of a people group that has very few churches, then workers should critically evaluate how they spend their time so that they are mobilizing outsiders to share the gospel among the people group.

In addition to increasing the quantity of witnesses, there is great need to improve the quality of how we are witnessing. It is invaluable to find one way to share the gospel so that more people can share the gospel. Everyone should have one way to share the gospel so they can easily share and easily train others. But we do not want to fall into the ditch of always sharing a dry, canned monologue. Key issues here are contextualizing the message for the listener and ongoing training of how to dialogue well in presentation.

Any3[1] is a dialogical presentation of the gospel contextualized for Muslims so that the witness interacts with Muslims to get beneath their surface understanding of their own religion to the roots of their desires and uncertainties. For Buddhist peoples some have adjusted Any3 to more of a Buddhist approach, or used a version of the Three Circles[2] presentation to deal with a root issue of suffering.

The advantage of using the Creation to Christ[3] type of chronological story presentation is that people are introduced to the concept of God by hearing about his actions and character throughout history. When properly trained, Creation to Christ involves true dialogue with the other person rather than becoming a long monologue.

Recent academic strides have brought practical means of how to share the gospel with an honor-shame perspective. Listeners in honor-shame cultures can more readily understand sin as dishonoring God as opposed what they might not understand about breaking moral rules they are not familiar with. Animists are more open to the gospel when the witness addresses their felt needs about their fear of spirits and what to do about their ancestors. These types of power-fear aspects of the gospel are also immediately applicable to those whose background is Buddhist, Muslim, and nominally atheist.

Some of the presentations above have aspects of honor-shame, power-fear, and guilt-innocence already built into the presentation. But witnesses themselves need a deeper training of understanding these root issues so they can dialogue at the heart level with people.

Our gospel message must be clear so people can understand the gospel for salvation. Further the gospel should be clear and holistic so that it encompasses all of our life. Too many churches have a weak and assumed understanding of the gospel so that it is more about the afterlife.

In addition to evangelism, a great need for establishing healthy, multiplying churches among UPGs is leadership training. Leadership training has been abundant in China for many years, but there is always a desire for more. Most of the UPG leaders do not desire to sit in the classroom for eight hours a day for multiple days. It is painful for farmers to sit in the classroom that long especially if the training is done in a second language to them or through a translator. Too often our training programs are filled with holes so that the learning leaks out.

The more effective training methods are those that are those that are interactive. Adult learners, especially the less educated, do better with

---

1. Shipman, *Any-3*.
2. Campbell, "Gospel Tool: 3 Circles."
3. "Creation to Christ."

role-plays, application of problem solving, and interacting with their specific cultural situations. When the teacher is able to facilitate discussion with Bible stories and life scenarios, learners stay awake as they are forced to truly interact with the content than sit back passively.

The top felt needs for UPG pastors I have interacted with are learning how to manage a church, helping their church members understand how to have healthy marriages and family, and giving them certified credentials of an official study program. A few other kinds of training are not felt needs until they actually experience a good training with them. These new felt needs are hermeneutics, storying, and song writing.

Pastors want a lot of content on theology and especially Bible teaching, but it all becomes rote regurgitation that does not affect their teaching until they get training and practice in basic hermeneutics. Some of the most effective and enjoyable courses are simply teaching and model hermeneutical tools of biblical interpretation, one at a time. Students prepare a 4 minute reduced version of their teaching and get feedback from their teachers and fellow students. Over and over proper biblical interpretation is practiced and reinforced so they truly know how to teach the Bible rather than random inspiration.

A third pressing need for reaching UPGs in China still continues to be heart language. Mandarin usage is increasing rapidly so that some people groups rarely use their traditional language. There is a growing need for bilingual materials. But there are still many people groups with large percentages of people who do not understand Mandarin.

The Bible is being translated into many languages across China, and still there are not enough translation projects and translation consultants. But real progress is being made in the form of Bible storying. In the past, translators worked hard to get Bible stories translated and recorded in heart languages, but sometimes even those recordings would not be used well. What is needed is not just stories but storying. The key is storytellers themselves. When storytellers truly understand the message and craft the way they tell the stories with more clarity, accuracy, and naturalness, storytelling becomes alive.

In a training not long ago, there were some minority group pastors who were part of a largely Han network. After working through the Bible story and acting it out, one of the pastors said in broken Mandarin, "This is the first time I have really understood the Bible for myself!"

If sometimes even pastors cannot understand Mandarin, then what about the local church member. Another church leader recalled the time that he used to sing Mandarin praise songs, " In my heart I knew I was praising God, but I had no idea the meaning of the actual words I was singing."

Healthy discipleship cannot happen if people do not understand the Bible for themselves.

The dire need for heart language Scripture, stories, and songs cannot be overstated. And now even in the remote villages, the UPGs are finally getting to the point where most people have smart phones. The church of China is only just now beginning to tap into the potential of gospel media. Some UPGs are already benefitting from apps, smaller sized media shared over social media, and the ability to target people with advanced analytics and marketing. Heart language needs are both low tech and high tech.

ESTABLISH AN ACCURATE SPOTLIGHT FOR A PERMANENT WITNESS AMONG UNENGAGED, UNREACHED PEOPLE GROUPS (UUPGS).

UUPGs are a type of UPG, but with more unique needs because no one is on the ground among them implementing a church planting strategy. Their great need is for a permanent witness among them and the key way for that to happen is for the church to know that the group exists. UUPGs do not need someone mishandling Matthew 24:14 to say that we need to share the gospel with the people group so that Christ will come back. UUPGs need a bright spotlight shone on them and more accurate information about who they are.

Some of the needed strategies toward these ends are not new at all, such as prayer. Prayer profiles for unreached people groups are probably at the top of ways that workers are called to these groups. The Joshua Project, *Operation China*[4], Top 30 UUPGs prayer books, and prayer calendars have all been worth every penny invested.

Mobilization events have also led to workers being sent out to UUPGs, but the success rate is much lower. Often commitments and adoptions have been pressured more by the peer pressure of the event rather the Holy Spirit. Mobilization events for UPGs might be more effective if they are prolonged prayer meetings geared toward a prayer movement more than recruitment.

As larger people groups become engaged, the average population size of UUPGs is getting smaller and smaller. People want to engage the low hanging fruit, but groups are more difficult to engage and we know much less information. Sometimes people pray about reaching a UUPG and move their lives to reach the group, only to find out that the group no longer exists or never existed. At this stage of UUPG work, there is a great need for more accurate information.

---

4. Hattaway, *Operation China*.

We no longer have to rely completely on expert linguists and researchers to give information on people groups. Linguists can train just about anyone to do the dialect survey work by sitting down with multiple sets of speakers to record a list of 100 words. Surveyors give the recordings to linguists who will then transcribe the phonetics list and provide analysis. Surveyors also gather information on the strength of the language, the local status of Christianity, and other demographics.

Further needed accuracy is with the name of the people groups. Linguistic research is helpful toward accuracy, but at times it is confusing to keep up with the consistent naming of people groups. Linguistic papers, people group databases, and different organizations sometimes use different naming systems especially when it comes to UUPGs. One simple way to help with consistency for the purpose of engagement would be for the people groups to adopt the naming system of the 56 official Chinese ethnicities so that databases for smaller people groups added on the larger naming system category. For example, the Sani would be called the Sani Yi so that it would be easier to identify a group as Yi, Tibetan, etc. In common conversation in Chinese, they usually say call themselves by this general name anyway unless they are speaking their heart language.

The thrust of each of these suggestions is to shine a brighter spotlight on the people group so they are known and found and prayed for by more people. These things lead UUPGs being engaged and reached.

One aspect of reaching the UPGs that we focus on should also be to cast the vision for our focus people to reach other UUPGs. If we, then, bring the UUPG responsibility into our focus, efforts toward shining a brighter and more accurate spotlight on these UUPGs will not take away from our efforts with our focus UPG. The people we minister to will catch our heart for the nations and be helped away from their own natural ethnocentric tendencies. The young churches of the UPG we minister to will greatly benefit from extensive prayer for these other people groups.

The vantage point of including UUPGs in our focus is synergistic rather than distracting.

ESTABLISH INDIGENOUS, CATALYTIC STRUCTURES AMONG REACHED PEOPLE GROUPS (RPGS).

I have spent a good portion of the chapter focusing on what foreign missionaries can do to reach unreached people groups, but the larger task at hand is to help China reach the UPGs of China and the world. Indeed, China has been sending workers Back to Jerusalem for over a decade and continuing that now even through alignment with Xi Jinping's One Belt, One Road. As China's global influence increase, so does the church of China's interest in reaching the people beyond their own city.

If the mobilization train is already moving, then why do we need to help? The church of China has a lot of the answers, but not all of them. They still need and want to learn things from foreign missionaries. Likewise, we have many things to learn from them as well.

This is very similar to the situation of the Antioch church in Acts 11. Barnabas did not plant the church there, but he went there to encourage and to teach. He reported all of the new and good things the church was doing, but he also sent for Paul to come teach them things they needed to learn. And ultimately, Antioch became known as the missionary base for Paul to reach from Jerusalem all the way to Illyricum and beyond.

Likewise, foreign workers among Chinese UPGs can serve the churches of Reached People Groups (RPGs) by encouraging, teaching, and equipping them.

First, we need to encourage churches for all of the good they are doing. Chinese churches tend to share the gospel very well. The church in eastern China has been growing rapidly for many years now. Church leaders have a great fervor for missions as they take initiatives to stage mobilization events and practical initiatives for taking the gospel all the way back around the world from the West onward to Jerusalem and the Muslim world. There are also newer initiatives, such as Mission China 2030 among the newer urban churches as they challenge themselves to call out foreign missionaries.

Another exciting phenomenon is that more and more churches are getting involved in human needs of their local communities. They are responding to disasters with skill and love. They are starting non-profit organizations to help the children and elderly of their community. They are working together to bring clean water, new clothes, and food to those who are needy. The church is living out the gospel truth of transformed lives as they love people, not merely as a platform to present the gospel, but because the gospel has changed their own hearts.

Second, we need to teach the churches of RPGs. Unfortunately, the dearth of good hermeneutics is not limited to the churches of UPGs. Missionaries and pastors need basic understanding of proper biblical interpretation so they can teach and so they can understand and appropriately apply Scripture to their own lives.

Similarly, biblical teaching on marriage and family is crucial to effective ministry as they reach out to UPGs. Too often missionaries leave their families in the cities from the east for months at a time in order to minister across the country. Many young singles are doing missions work, but they have not seen good models of appropriate relationships. Teaching and application is important, but much more can also be learned by spending time with foreign husbands, wives, fathers, and mothers who have a biblical foundation of marriage and family.

Another important thing to teach RPGs is a more holistic discipleship that addresses the head, hands, and heart. Discipleship often just addresses the "head" aspect of our lives with more knowledge. Many RPG Christians feel inadequate to share the gospel because they do not know enough so they are not at the high standard they would like to be. But discipleship that does not lead to the "hands" aspect of obedience will effectively become a hypocritical discipleship. Furthermore, we must not neglect the "heart" aspect of discipleship that transforms not just our behavior but our desire to know God, love God, and honor God. Each of these things are important aspects to help RPGs follow Christ better and reach out to UPGs more effectively.

Third, we have the ability to equip RPGs in the ministry skills they need to cross cultures to share the gospel. Many RPGs (including and especially the RPGs of the West) are unaware of their ethnocentrism and attempt to cross cultures with an inhibiting pride. We can help with awareness of other cultures through classroom teaching about culture and religion. But crossing cultures is more caught than it is taught. Crossing cultures is primarily a heart issue. We must be willing to listen, to learn, to explore, and to fail. Cross-cultural adaptation happens incrementally through reflection and debriefing.

Thus, it takes more than a book and a class to equip someone in crossing cultures. It takes more than a five-day trip. Helping people cross cultures requires us to have the expectations of the time, patience, coaching, and encouraging needed for someone who has lived in a nearly monocultural city.

We need to equip the churches of China with skills and structures that they do not have. Only in the past few years have more Han started learning the minority languages of UPGs. Many of them struggle because while they and their sending churches are some of the few that gain the vision for learning the heart language, the sending churches do not always understand the time and effort it takes for them to learn the language. Fluency cannot be expected in six months especially when your sending church also wants you to be sharing the gospel ten times each week.

Other skills and networks needed are business training, equipping to be a translator or story crafting facilitator, a music and media network, and how to coach other missionaries. Churches need help in setting up their own mission sending organizations and processes. Often churches are sending troubled kids to mission training centers because that is one answer to help their kids to be in a good environment. Instead, churches need to have processes in place to send the ones who are called by God rather than just called by their parents.

CONCLUSION

If all the foreign missionaries left China today, the church of China could continue the work of reaching the people groups of China. But it would take many more years. The church of China would continue to make the mistakes that we have already learned from. We have the vantage point of experience. We have the vantage point of proximity. Yet if we focus too tightly only on the UPGs we are called to, we will limit our field of vision to the point of unwittingly crippling ourselves.

China is ready to reach the UPGs of China and the world. The foreign missionaries working with the UPGs are at a critical juncture to help make that happen.

Chapter 12

Reaching Northwest China

TABOR LAUGHLIN

INTRODUCTION

NW China is becoming an increasingly significant region in China for many reasons. The Chinese government is focusing on the "Belt and Road" initiative, which also includes NW China. Chinese house churches around the country have been striving to send Chinese missionaries to serve along the ancient Silk Road. This ancient Silk Road not only includes countries west of China, but also includes NW China. So many Chinese "missionaries" from churches in eastern China have been sent to NW China to plant churches and reach minority people groups there. In addition, though there are many minority peoples [non-Han Chinese] in NW China, there is a continued need for foreign missionaries and Chinese believers to not only minister to the minority groups in NW China, but also do discipleship and evangelism within the China majority people group Han Chinese population in NW China. Also needed are people to help the relatively weak house churches in NW China by helping mentor the pastors or being involved in any form of theological education.

Belt and Road Initiative and NW China

As far as more recent Chinese developments are concerned, the Chinese government is implementing the YiDaiYiLu (一带一路) "One Belt One Road" policy. More recently this has been renamed as the "Belt and Road Initiative." The idea is that the Chinese government—led by President Xi Jinping—will strengthen trade between China and countries in Central Asia, South Asia, Eastern Europe, the Middle East, and Africa. The Chinese government aims to develop the infrastructure between China and the other participating countries. Roads and high-speed trains are to be built. Airports and power plants are to be constructed.

Recently there was an informative article in *The Atlantic* on the "Belt and Road" initiative.[1] The article mentions how this initiative was critical in turning the Pakistani town of Gwadar from a small poor fishing village into a place with new hotels and 1,800 miles of "superhighway and high-speed railway" to connect Gwadar to Western China. An estimated $300 million has already been spent on the "Belt and Road" initiative, with another $1 trillion being spent in the upcoming decade. The CIA reports how 92 countries counted China as their largest export or import partners in 2015; in the same year, only 57 countries counted the U.S. as their largest export or import partners. The Chinese government uses its money and resources to win the favor of these other countries. President Xi understands that the "Belt and Road" initiative ultimately helps China flourish economically. This initiative means that China and these other countries do not need to rely as much on trade with the U.S. anymore. Rather, these other countries will be relying more than ever on trade with China. It is estimated that China spends about $150 billion per year in the 68 countries that at present are involved in this "initiative."

NW China is relevant to the "Belt and Road" plan for several reasons. NW China is the part of China that is closest to these other countries involved in the "Belt and Road Initiative." To get from eastern or southern China to these other countries, it is necessary to go through NW China. And to deliver goods from these other countries into China, it is necessary to go through NW China. NW China is the gateway to these other countries involved in the "Belt and Road Initiative." So the Chinese government is pouring in lots of money into developing NW China.

The "Belt and Road" initiative seemingly will open up some doors for ministry in NW China. Greater infrastructure in NW China will greatly shrink the vast and expansive region of NW China, which is primarily

---

1. Manuel, "China Belt and Road."

characterized by immense deserts and towering mountains. It will be easier and faster to travel from one city to another. High-speed trains are now connecting many large cities in NW China, and roads and trains will be utilized to more significantly connect all areas of NW China. NW China is now being seen as a more important and strategic region by the Chinese government. Similarly, more missionaries or Chinese believers may be interested to minister in NW China, as a result of the area's speedy development. And there will be more possible positions for missionaries to serve in NW China, because as the region develops, there will be more jobs for missionaries to have. Missionaries will be able to find legitimate jobs not only in capital cities in NW China, but also in smaller cities and towns. May the Lord use the self-serving plans of the Chinese government in the "Belt and Road" initiative for the spread of the gospel in NW China and beyond!

The Ancient Silk Road

There is a large movement of Chinese Christians from mainland China moving west along the ancient Silk Road to take the gospel back the way it came. These Chinese missionaries go into western China, and into Central Asia (i.e. Pakistan, Afghanistan, Kazakhstan), India, Eastern Europe, the Middle East, and North Africa and eventually back to Israel. Basically these regions—including NW China—are a huge part of the so-called "10/40 Window," which constitutes the area between Africa and East Asia and is the area of the most "unreached" peoples in the world. In other words, these areas are greatly Muslim and Buddhist and strongly antagonistic towards Christianity. This part of the world is incredibly dark spiritually.

Other than the majority ethnic group (Han) population, which makes up 91 percent of the total China population, NW China is also filled with many minority people groups. Some of these are: Hui (Muslim); Uyghur (Muslim); Salar (Muslim); and, various kinds of Tibetans (Buddhist). Though minority peoples in NW China are plentiful, most of the people in larger cities in NW China are the majority Han. As previously mentioned, the Han constitute 91 percent of the overall population in China, and also make up a large percentage of people in NW China. This being the case, in smaller cities and towns in NW China usually there will be a greater concentration of other minority people groups. And this is the case the further west in NW China that one moves. For example, small towns and large cities in Shaanxi province—the farthest east province in NW China—almost entirely consist of Han Chinese. But in provinces further west—like Qinghai and Xinjiang—there will be larger cities that consist of almost entirely minority peoples (i.e. Kashgar in Xinjiang). This being said, all capital cities in NW China (Urumqi, Xining, Lanzhou, Yinchuan, Xian)—though they are the largest cities in their provinces—consist of a high proportion of majority Han people, rather than minority people groups. This is a reality because the Chinese government in Beijing for decades has sent many Han Chinese from eastern China to work in capital cities in NW China and help lead companies and local governments, and help balance the local minority group population with a larger Han population.

Role of Those Ministering in NW China

There is great need for those ministering in NW China to be involved in evangelism and discipleship. This could be happening within a minority people group, or in ministering to Han Chinese. There are relatively few people in NW China who go to a church and consider themselves as "Christian," compared to those in other parts of China. It is necessary as a missionary or other minister of the gospel in that part of the country to be active in sharing the gospel with locals. We are to be bold in proclaiming the good news of Jesus Christ. May we be like Paul, who writes, "Woe to me if I do not preach the gospel!" (1 Cor. 9:16) At the same time, though there can be benefits to sharing the gospel randomly with taxi drivers or people on the street in NW China, it is usually advisable to share one's life and faith through close relationships with locals (1 Thess. 2:8). In China, it is illegal and heavily discouraged for missionaries or Chinese believers to hand out Bibles or gospel tracts on the street. Rather, I have found that the most effective form of evangelism in China is through relationships. Through meeting one-on-one regularly with locals, or in smaller groups, it is easier to have a greater spiritual impact on the locals while also not getting in trouble with the local police.

The house churches in NW China are not as developed or strong as those in other parts of China. Those few locals who are involved in local house churches may completely lack having some kind of "mentor" or "discipler" over them. This is a huge contribution that those ministering in NW China can still make: Evangelism towards the many lost in NW China, or being involved in discipleship of locals who profess to be Christians. Most Chinese churches—just like many other churches around the world—struggle with having any kind of habits or atmosphere of discipleship. Chinese may go to the house churches weekly, but have no spiritual growth over many years because no one in the church is investing in them in a deeper way. This is a way that missionaries or Chinese brothers and sisters can fill the gap for these Chinese believers, to disciple Chinese who profess to be Christians.

There is a great need for those ministering in NW China to be trying to reach the Han Chinese. Yes, there are many missionaries in NW China. However, most of them are reaching the minority people groups in the area. Very few of them are reaching the majority Han in the area, or trying to work together with Han house churches. This should not be the case, as there are still many Han Chinese living in NW China. And the Han Chinese in NW China are very far from being considered as a "reached" group. Among the Han Chinese masses in most areas in NW China, local Christians are very hard to find and very much the minority.

Missionaries or Chinese serving in the area can help open the eyes of local house church believers. In NW China, though there are an abundance of minority peoples, the local house churches generally have little desire to try to minister to these nearby minority groups. We can help encourage the local Chinese to see the need to reach out to those minorities around them. These Chinese often can be most effective to reach the minorities there, because they already speak a common language—Chinese—as most of those belonging to minority groups.

There is also a need for deeper theological training in NW China. Many of the house church pastors in NW China are uneducated and have often not even gone to high school. At present, there are a growing number of solid underground theological training centers or Bible schools scattered around most of China. Praise God for this reality, and may this trend continue. There are copious underground theological centers in cities like Beijing, Shanghai, Wenzhou, Chengdu, or even Xian. But—particularly north and west of Xian—there are very few established and well-organized theological training centers in NW China. The pastors in NW China often must travel to other parts of China or overseas for theological training; this can be costly and burdensome, and require the pastor leaving his family in China. Maybe some missionaries or Chinese in NW China can help local Chinese house churches set up Bible training schools in their cities. If the missionaries help play a part in getting the Bible school set up and giving initial guidance, then eventually the missionaries ideally should let the local Chinese believers take over leadership and supervision of the Bible school. This does not mean that the Bible training school should look exactly like one from foreign countries. But in some situations missionaries may help in getting the training school up and running, and then pass it on to locals.

Those ministering in NW China may also play a role in helping mobilize more Chinese missionaries from house churches in NW China to minister in other parts of the world. Most house churches sending Chinese missionaries globally are in eastern or southern China. There are fewer Chinese missionaries being sent from NW China. But local Chinese from Xinjiang province may be better fit to serve as missionaries in Central Asia. The Uyghur and other Muslim minority groups in Xinjiang are similar to the Muslim peoples who live in Central Asia. The climate, terrain, food and many cultural aspects are similar in Xinjiang and much of Central Asia. There should be less culture shock for Chinese missionaries who move from Xinjiang to Central Asia. And as Xinjiang borders Central Asia, it is cheaper and more convenient to move there.

Conclusion

The spiritual needs in NW China are extensive. And it is not just the needs in reaching the many minority people groups there, though that is also important. As far as the overall population in NW China goes, the majority of the people are still normal Chinese people (Han), not minority peoples. Both these Han Chinese and minority people groups there are for the most part completely void of personally knowing a Christian in their life. There is a need for ambassadors of Christ bringing the gospel to them and developing tight relationships with these people. And for those in house churches in NW China, they often need to be discipled. And an even greater need is for those ministering in NW China to mentor local house church pastors and to be involved in some form of theological training in NW China. And as mentioned before, recent economic development and improved infrastructure in NW China has also opened the door for providing many opportunities for ministers of the gospel to live and minister.

Bibliography

All Girls Allowed. "Gendercide China Statistics." http://www.allgirlsallowed.org/gendercide-china-statistics.
Bellon, Emmanuel O. *Leading Financial Sustainability in Theological Institutions: The African Perspective.* Eugene, OR: Pickwick Publications, 2017.
BMJ Publishing Group. "China's Excess Males, Sex Selective Abortion, and One Child Policy: Analysis of Data from 2005 National Intercensus Survey." https://www.bmj.com/content/338/bmj.b1211.full.
Bosch, David J. *Transforming Mission: Paradigm Shifts in Theology of Mission.* Maryknoll, NY: Orbis Books, 1991.
Bristow, Michael. "Has China's One-Child Policy Worked?" http://news.bbc.co.uk/2/hi/7000931.stm, 2007.
Campbell, Fred. "Gospel Tool: 3 Circles." *Mission Frontiers Sending Base Movements: Equipping Local Churches to Reach Their Communities and the Nations,* 2016.
Chao, Jonathan. "Towards an Evangelical Theology in Totalitarian Cultures With Special Reference to Socialist China." *Theology in Asian Contexts,* 2010.
Charlotte Lozier Institute. "A Half Century of Hope, A Legacy of Life and Love: Pregnancy Center Service Report." Third Edition, 2018. http://lozierinstitute.org/wp-content/uploads/2018/09/A-Half-Century-of-Hope-A-Legacy-of-Life-and-Love-FULL.pdf.
The China NGO Project. "Government Cartoon Portrays 'Foreign NGOs' as National Security Threat." http://www.chinafile.com/ngo/latest/government-cartoon-portrays-foreign-ngos-national-security-concern.
The China NGO Project. "Law of the People's Republic of China on Administration of Activities of Overseas Nongovernmental Organizations in the Mainland of China," April 28, 2016, as posted at. http://www.chinafile.com/ngo/laws-regulations/law-of-peoples-republic-of-china-administration-of-activities-of-overseas.
The China NGO Project. "Will 2018 Be the Year of a Silent Foreign NGO Exodus?" May 23, 2018. http://www.chinafile.com/ngo/latest/will-2018-be-year-of-silent-foreign-ngo-exodus.
ChinaSource. "Seven Trends Impacting Foreign Christians in China." https://www.chinasource.org/resource-library/books/7-trends-impacting-foreign-christians-in-china.
Chow, Alexander. *Chinese Public Theology: Generational Shifts and Confucian Imagination in Chinese Christianity.* Oxford: Oxford University Press, 2018.

Coleman, Priscilla K. "Abortion and Mental Health: Quantitative Synthesis and Analysis of Research Published 1995–2009." *British Journal of Psychiatry*: 119(3), 2011.

"Creation to Christ." https://c2cstory.com/the-story.

Cron, Ian Morgan and Suzanne Stabile. *The Road Back to You: An Enneagram Journey to Self-Discovery*. Downers Grove, IL: Inter-Varsity Press, 2016.

Dowley, Tim, John H. Y. Briggs, Robert Dean Linder, and David F. Wright. *Introduction to the History of Christianity*. Minneapolis: Fortress Press, 2006.

Doyle, G. Wright. "A Theology for House Churches." http://www.reachingchineseworldwide.org/wright-doyle/articles/christianity/a-theology-for-house-churches.

Doyle, G. Wright. *Reaching Chinese Worldwide*. Durham, NC: TorchFlame Books, 2013.

The Economist. "Gendercide." https://www.economist.com/leaders/2010/03/04/gendercide.

Fielding, Charles. *Preach and Heal: A Biblical Model for Missions*. Richmond, VA: International Mission Board, 2008.

Fredenburg, Michaelene. *Changed*. San Diego, CA: Perspectives, 2013.

Fulton, Brent. *China's Urban Christians: A Light That Cannot Be Hidden*. Eugene, OR: Pickwick Publications, 2015.

Fulton, Brent. "Journeying with the Church in China." ChinaSource, March 2017. https://www.chinasource.org/resource-library/chinasource-quarterlies/journeying-with-the-church-in-china.

Fulton, Brent. "Will China Become Generous?" *ChinaSource*, December 7, 2016. https://www.chinasource.org/blog/posts/will-china-become-generous.

Gilliland, Burl E., and Richard K. James. *Crisis Intervention Strategies*. 8th ed. Boston: Cengage Learning, 2016.

Guttmacher Institute. "Facts on Induced Abortion in the United States," May 2011. http://www.guttmacher.org/pubs/fb_induced_abortion.html.

Guttmacher Institute. "Induced Abortion Worldwide." https://www.guttmacher.org/fact-sheet/induced-abortion-worldwide.

Hattaway, Paul. *Operation China: Introducing All the Peoples of China*. Pasadena, Calif..: William Carey Library, 2000.

Hyatt, Irwin T. "Protestant Missions in China, 1877–1890: The Institutionalization of Good Works." In *American Missionaries in China: Papers from Harvard Seminars*. Ed. Kwang-Ching Liu. Cambridge, MA: Harvard East Asian Research Center, 1966.

Johnson, Ian. *The Souls of China*. New York: Pantheon Books, 2017.

Kaiser, Andrew T. "Chinese Christians Preparing for 'New Normal.'" *The Gospel Coalition*. March 2, 2017. https://www.thegospelcoalition.org/article/chinese-christians-preparing-for-new-normal/, Date Accessed: June 7, 2018.

Kaiser, Andrew T. *Encountering China: The Evolution of Timothy Richard's Missionary Thought (1870–1891)*. Eugene, OR: Pickwick Publications, 2019.

Kang, C., Y. Wang. "Sex Ratio at Birth." In: Theses Collection of 2001 National Family Planning and Reproductive Health Survey. Beijing: China Population Publishing House: 88–98. (referenced in NEJM), 2003.

Keller, Timothy J. *Center Church*. Grand Rapids: Zondervan, 2012.

Kilner, John. *Why The Church Needs Bioethics*. Zondervan, 2011.

Klusendorf, Scott. "Defending Your Prolife Views in Five Minutes Or Less." In John Ensor and Scott Klusendorf, *Stand for Life*. Peabody, MA: Hendrickson Publishers, 2012.

Kwan, Simon S. M. and Archie C. C. Lee. "Theological Education in Hong Kong: A Postcolonial Reading." In *Handbook of Theological Education in World Christianity: Theological Perspectives-Regional Surveys-Ecumenical Trends*, edited by Dietrich Werner, David Esterline, and Namsoon Kang. Oxford: Regnum, 2010.

Lampton, David. *Following the Leader: Ruling China from Deng Xiaoping to Xi Jinping*. Berkeley and Los Angeles: University of California Press, 2014.

Lanfranchi, Angela, Ian Gentles, and Elizabeth Ring-Cassidy. *Complications: Abortion's Impact on Women*. Toronto: The deVerber Institute of Bioethics and Social Research, 2013.

Laven, Mary. *Mission to China: Matteo Ricci and the Jesuit Encounter with the East*. London: Faber and Faber, 2011.

Li, Fan, as quoted in Evan Osnos, "Five Things You Need to Know about Faith in China." *On Faith*. https://www.onfaith.co/onfaith/2014/05/13/five-things-you-need-to-know-about-faith-in-china/32061.

M, Tim. "A New Way of Partnership: Directional Koinonia." In Kingdom Pursuit: Exploring the Many Facets of Missions, edited by Carl D. Chaplin and Sue Harris, 152–67. Lawrenceville: CDM, 2017.

Ma, Li, and Jin Li. *Surviving the State, Remaking the Church: A Sociological Portrait of Christians in China*. Eugene, OR: Pickwick Publications, 2017.

Ma, Mary. *The Chinese Exodus: A Theology of Migration, Urbanism and Alienation in Contemporary China*. Eugene, OR: Wipf and Stock Publishers, 2018.

Manuel, Anja. "China Belt and Road." *The Atlantic*, October 17, 2017. https://www.theatlantic.com/international/archive/2017/10/china-belt-and-road/542667.

Moore, Russell. *Adopted for Life: The Priority of Adoption for Christian Families and Churches*. Wheaton, Ill.: Crossway Books, 2009.

Nakah, Victor. "Theological Education and the Church in Africa" In Kingdom Pursuit: Exploring the Many Facets of Missions, edited by Carl D. Chaplin and Sue Harris, 187–94. Lawrenceville: CDM, 2017.

Park, James. "Theological Education in Asia Since World War II," 2014.

Poon, Michael Nai Chiu. "The Association for Theological Education in South East Asia, 1959– 2002: A Pilgrimage in Theological Education." In *Supporting Asian Christianity's Transition from Mission to Church: A History of the Foundation for Theological Education in South East Asia*, edited by Samuel C Pearson. Grand Rapids: Eerdmans, 2010.

Reardon, David C. *Aborted Women, Silent No More*. Chicago: Loyola University Press, 1997.

Shieh, Shawn. "Remaking China's Civil Society in the Xi Jinping Era," August 1, 2018. *ChinaFile*. http://www.chinafile.com/reporting-opinion/viewpoint/remaking-chinas-civil-society-xi-jinping-era.

Shipman, Mike. *Any-3: Anyone, Anywhere, Anytime*. Monument, Colo.: WIGTake Resources, 2013.

Stark, Rodney. *The Rise of Christianity: How the Obscure, Marginal Jesus Movement Became the Dominant Religious Force in the Western World in a Few Centuries*. San Francisco: HarperSanFrancisco, 1997.

Stark, Rodney, and Xiuhua Wang. *A Star in the East: The Rise of Christianity in China*. West Conshohocken: Templeton Press, 2015.

Steffen, Tom. *The Facilitator Era*. Eugene, OR: Wipf and Stock Publishers, 2011.

Stephen Z. "The Expectations of the Chinese Church." ChinaSource, March 2017. https://www.chinasource.org/resource-library/articles/the-expectations-of-the-chinese-church.

Swells in the Middle Kingdom. "The Challenges of Localization: Why Localize Now?" ChinaSource, Dec 9, 2016. https://www.chinasource.org/resource-library/blog-entries/the-challenges-of-localization.

Towson, Jeffrey, and Jonathan Woetzel. *The 1-Hour China Book: Two Peking University Professors Explain All of China Business in Six Short Stories*. Cayman Islands: Towson Group LLC, 2013.

U.S. Congressional-Executive Commission on China. Annual Report, 2008. https://www.gpo.gov/fdsys/pkg/CHRG-110hhrg45233/pdf/CHRG-110hhrg45233.pdf.

Wang, Jianguo. "China and the Church in China, Part Two: Kings and the Gospel." China Partnership. http://www.chinapartnership.org/blog/2018/2/china-and-the-church-in-china-part-2-kings-and-the-gospel.

Weber, Charles. "'Abolish This Great Evil': Chinese Christians' Opposition to Opium Trafficking." In *Shaping Christianity in Greater China: Indigenous Christians in Focus*. ed. Paul Woods. Oxford: Regnum Books International, 2017.

Women's Rights without Frontiers. "Forced Abortion is not a Choice." http://www.womensrightswithoutfrontiers.org/index.php?nav=female_suicide.

Xi, Lian. *The Conversion of Missionaries: Liberalism in American Protestant Missions in China, 1907–1932*. University Park, PA: Pennsylvania State University, 1997.

Xi, Lian. *Redeemed by Fire: The Rise of Popular Christianity in Modern China*. New Haven: Yale University Press, 2010.

Xi, Wu, and TT. "China Emerging as a Mission Sending Country." ChinaSource, December 2016. https://www.chinasource.org/resource-library/articles/china-emerging-as-a-mission-sending-country.

Y-Wang. "A Glance at People with Disabilities in China." ChinaSource, March 7, 2016. http://www.chinasource.org/resource-library/articles/a-glance-at-people-with-disabilities-in-china.

Yang, Fenggang. *Religion in China: Survival and Revival Under Communist Rule*. New York: Oxford University Press, 2012.

Yang, Fenggang. "Cultural Dynamics in China: Today and in 2020." *Asia Policy*. 4:41–52, 2007.

www.ingramcontent.com/pod-product-compliance
Lightning Source LLC
Chambersburg PA
CBHW050822160426
43192CB00010B/1854